D0645607

A. S. Byatt

A. S. BYATT

A. S. Byatt

Richard Todd

Northcote House

in association with
The British Council

First published in 1997 by Northcote House Publishers Ltd, Plymbridge House, Estover Road, Plymouth PL6 7PY, United Kingdom
Tel: +44 (0) 1752 202368. Fax +44 (0) 1752 202330

British Library Cataloguing-in-Publication Data
A catalogue record for this book is available from the British Library

ISBN 0 7463 0792 6

Typeset by Florencetype Ltd, Stoodleigh, Devon
Printed and bound in the United Kingdom

dit is Winnies boekje

Contents

Acknowledgements and Note

Grateful thanks are due to the following for information, for assistance with queries, and for other forms of cooperation: Jonathan Burnham and Jenny Uglow of Chatto & Windus Ltd; Carmen Callil, formerly of Chatto & Windus Ltd (an imprint of Random House UK Ltd); Frances Coady and Jörg Hensgen of Vintage (an imprint of Random House UK Ltd); John Cody of Random House Australia Pty Ltd; Michael Sissons of the Peters Fraser & Dunlop Group Ltd; and Nicki Kennedy of the Intercontinental Literary Agency associated with the Peters Fraser & Dunlop Group Ltd.

The author and publisher are grateful to A. S. Byatt and to both above-named divisions of Random House UK Ltd for permission to quote from the works of A. S. Byatt. In both conversation and correspondence I have learnt a great deal from Byatt's translators into Danish, French, and German: they are, respectively, Claus Bech, Jean-Louis Chevalier, and Melanie Walz. I would also like to thank Gill Marsden for sending me much that would not otherwise have come my way, and Patricia Sullivan, a student at St John's University, New York, for allowing me to consult a detailed bibliography compiled by her for a term project. Thanks, too, as always, to my colleagues in Amsterdam: in particular Theo Bögels, Daniel Carroll, and Rod Lyall for support and comment, and most of all Christien Franken for bibliographical advice, assistance, and encouragement.

The reader of any essay of this kind, concerning as it does the work of a writer still very much at the height of her powers, may legitimately wonder how far the contents have been *authorized* by the subject. I ought therefore to make clear that from the outset it was agreed between all parties concerned, including the General Editor of the *Writers and their Work* Series, Isobel

Armstrong (to whom I am most grateful for commissioning this study) that A. S. Byatt would read a penultimate draft prior to publication, but only with an eye to correcting any errors of fact. This she has kindly done; and indeed I am delighted to have this opportunity of acknowledging an immense personal debt, for she has shown me (as she has many other former students) friendship, inspiration, and example over a long period. While I am therefore confident that there is general agreement between us over most issues of interpretation and judgement concerning her work, I want to emphasize that A. S. Byatt has not in any way sought to influence the contents of this essay, and so I take full responsibility for the interpretations and judgements that follow.

Richard Todd

Amsterdam
August 1996

Biographical Outline

1936   Antonia Susan Drabble born in Sheffield on 24 August, eldest daughter of John Drabble, a barrister, and Marie *née* Bloor, a schoolteacher. Later attended Sheffield High School and The Mount School, York, a Quaker foundation.

1954–7   Read English at Newnham College, Cambridge.

1957–9   Postgraduate study at Bryn Mawr College, Pennsylvania, and Somerville College, Oxford.

1959   Married I. C. R. Byatt; marriage dissolved in 1969.

1960   Birth of a daughter, Antonia Byatt.

1961   Birth of a son, Charles Byatt.

1962–71   Taught in the Extra-Mural Department of London University.

1964   *Shadow of a Sun* (reissued in 1991 as *The Shadow of the Sun*).

1965   *Degrees of Freedom: The Novels of Iris Murdoch* (re-issued in 1994 as *Degrees of Freedom: The Early Novels of Iris Murdoch*). Taught at the Central School of Art and Design, London (until 1969).

1967   *The Game.*

1969   Married Peter J. Duffy.

1970   *Wordsworth and Coleridge in their Time* (reissued in 1989 as *Unruly Times: Wordsworth and Coleridge in their Time*). Birth of a daughter, Isabel Duffy.

1972   Appointed to full-time Lectureship in English and American Literature at University College London. Charles Byatt killed in a road accident.

1973   Birth of a daughter, Miranda Duffy.

1974   Appointed a Booker Prize judge for that year. Membership of BBC Social Effects of Television Advisory Group (until 1977).

1976	*Iris Murdoch* (British Council's first Writers and their Work series).
1978	*The Virgin in the Garden.* Membership of Board of Communications and Cultural Studies, Council for National Academic Awards (CNAA) (until 1984).
1979	Edited and introduced George Eliot's *The Mill on the Floss* for Penguin Classics.
1981	Promoted to Senior Lectureship at UCL.
1983	Retired from academic life to write full-time. Elected Fellow of the Royal Society of Literature.
1985	*Still Life.* Membership of Board of Creative and Performing Arts, CNAA (until 1987).
1986–8	Chairman of Society of Authors.
1987	*Sugar and Other Stories.* Membership of Kingman Committee on the teaching of the English language (until 1988). Hon. D.Litt., University of Bradford.
1990	Appointed a CBE for her work as a writer. Awarded the *Irish Times*/Aer Lingus International Fiction Prize, the Eurasian Regional Award of the Commonwealth Writers Prize, and the Booker Prize for Fiction for *Possession: A Romance. Possession* also shortlisted for the Whitbread Award. Co-edited, with Nicholas Warren, *George Eliot: Selected Essays, Poems and Other Writings.*
1991	*Passions of the Mind: Selected Writings.* Hon. D.Litt., Universities of Durham and York.
1992	*Angels and Insects.* Hon. D.Litt., University of Nottingham.
1993	*The Matisse Stories.* Hon. D.Litt., University of Liverpool.
1994	*The Djinn in the Nightingale's Eye.* Hon. D.Litt., University of Portsmouth.
1995	With Ignês Sodré, *Imagining Characters.* Hon D.Litt., University of London.
1996	*Babel Tower.*

Abbreviations and References

AI   *Angels and Insects* (London: Vintage, 1993)

BT   *Babel Tower* (London: Chatto & Windus, 1996)

DF   *Degrees of Freedom: The Early Novels of Iris Murdoch* (London: Vintage, 1994)

DNE   *The Djinn in the Nightingale's Eye* (London: Vintage, 1995)

EW   Eleanor Wachtell, interview with A. S. Byatt in *Writers & Company in Conversation with Eleanor Wachtell* (San Diego, New York, and London: Harcourt Brace & Co., 1994), 77–89

Fdj   *Le Fantôme de juillet* ('The July Ghost'), trans. Jean-Louis Chevalier (Paris: Éditions des Cendres, 1991)

G.   *The Game* (London: Vintage, 1992)

IC   (With Ignês Sodré), *Imagining Characters: Six Conversations about Women Writers* (London: Chatto & Windus, 1995)

JD   Juliet Dusinberre, interview with A. S. Byatt in Janet Todd (ed.), *Women Writers Talking* (New York: Holmes & Meier, 1983), 181–95

MS   *The Matisse Stories* (London: Vintage, 1994)

NT   Nicolas Tredell, interview with A. S. Byatt in *Conversations with Critics* (Manchester: Carcanet, 1994), 58–74

P.   *Possession: A Romance* (London: Vintage, 1991)

PM   *Passions of the Mind: Selected Writings* (London: Vintage, 1993)

SL   *Still Life* (London: Vintage, 1995)

SOS   *Sugar and Other Stories* (London: Penguin, 1988)

STS   *The Shadow of the Sun* (first published as *Shadow of a Sun*) (London: Vintage, 1991)

VG   *The Virgin in the Garden* (London: Vintage, 1994)

1

Introduction: Global Writer, Thinking Characters

The year 1990 was A. S. Byatt's *annus mirabilis*. In it she published her fifth novel, *Possession*, and won the £20,000 Booker Prize. The publication of *Possession* quickly brought Byatt world-wide renown, and over the next few years it prompted a complete reappraisal of her work. Not since Salman Rushdie and *Midnight's Children* in 1981 had Booker success so transformed a writer's career.

It has since come to seem that, as with Rushdie, Byatt had produced a novel for the times. Unlike Rushdie, for whom the Booker Prize actually launched a very different kind of career, Byatt had already established herself steadily since the late 1960s as a writer with a small but literary-minded following. She had begun an academic career that for a while took on a part-time character in the higher education sector as she brought up a young family. She was involved in university teaching and research from 1972 until 1983, when she retired to devote herself full-time to writing. She has long had a high profile in the media and in public life generally, and has always attracted an unusually high proportion of male readers. In this she is rather like Iris Murdoch, about whom she first published a strong and original book as early as 1965, the year after her own début as a novelist.

Possession quickly became a quite spectacular international success, a *livre de chevet* that was both admired and celebrated because it had somehow achieved what all serious writers yearn for, which is an appeal to a popular readership that does not compromise intellectual standards or aspiration. Byatt's formula remains as evasive and beguiling as that of Umberto Eco, whose international success with *The Name of the Rose*, a decade or so earlier, has since prompted frequent comparisons with Byatt and *Possession*.

World-wide English-language sales of *Possession* in both hardback and paperback six years after initial publication may be conservatively estimated at well over half a million, with total sales (including translations) approaching the million mark. Five years after the book's first appearance, the Vintage paperback reprint was still selling well. In Australia, Britain's main export market, a country with a third of Britain's population, Vintage paperback sales have now exceeded the highest estimates of hardback sales in Britain. Most amazing of all was *Possession*'s success in the USA, a market that is notoriously volatile and unpredictable for contemporary British fiction. Shortly after its US publication in the spring of 1991, weekly hardback sales were reported as being between 7,500 and 10,000, and total hardback sales are certain to have exceeded 100,000. At public readings of her work all over the world, in a decade in which the cult of the living writer has become unusually vigorous, Byatt attracts large audiences, made up of a higher proportion of women than formerly constituted her readership. Her work is widely discussed informally in reading clubs in Britain and elsewhere.

By December 1995 *Possession* had been translated into sixteen languages, including Japanese, Korean, Bulgarian, and Russian; Portuguese translation rights had been sold in Brazil. The fortunes of literature in translation are always mixed, but in several European countries Byatt's novel inspired translations of real distinction. Three enjoyed a particularly high profile. *Possession*, the French-language version of Jean-Louis Chevalier (the dedicatee of *Angels and Insects*), won the national Prix Baudelaire in 1994. Claus Bech's translation into Danish, *Besættelse*, was even shortlisted for the EU's Aristeion Prize, the citation describing it as 'brilliant and satisfying', and asserting that it 'sets a new standard for the translation of literature into Danish'. Melanie Walz's German translation, *Besessen*, achieved astonishing sales, comparable to the British hardback original figures. The Danish- and German-language cognate forms of the title, unavailable in French, allow the compelling suggestion of a sense of drivenness coupled with all the other aspects of 'possession' – financial, sexual, biographical, literary – that Byatt has subsequently stressed in interviews. The best translators have on various occasions described themselves as having been led back to their own cultural mainsprings to seek literary equivalents, allusions, and intellectual backgrounds. Bibliographical studies of contemporary literary fiction in English suggest that the Nordic countries, especially Denmark, are (along with the Low Countries) the most fruitful repositories of translation. The Danish, German, and French translations were evidently prepared with such care that the success of *Possession* in various European cultures must be ascribed to different forces in each case.

Whatever these forces may be, and they will be considered in due course, Byatt's subsequent collections of short stories and novellas *Angels and Insects* (1992), *The Matisse Stories* (1993), and *The Djinn in the Nightingale's Eye* (1994) have undoubtedly profited from the success of *Possession*. By December 1995 they were available in eight, ten, and six languages respectively.

Nor has the international breakthrough been a one-way traffic: Chevalier's French translations of *Le Sucre* (consisting of the title story only), and *Le Fantôme de juillet* (consisting of 'The July Ghost' and 'Precipice-Encurled'), were so handsomely produced by the Parisian publisher Éditions des Cendres that they inspired Chatto & Windus to find the striking formats used for *The Matisse Stories* and *The Djinn in the Nightingale's Eye*. It is also certain that *Possession* exercised a retrospective effect: by 1995 all Byatt's previous fiction had been reprinted by Vintage, with the exception of *Sugar and Other Stories* (1987), to which Penguin still held the rights. Post-*Possession* sales of these earlier titles in Britain and its main export markets have in virtually every case exceeded ten times the original hardback sales.

It is evidently pointless to try to ignore the watershed formed by *Possession* in A. S. Byatt's writing career. Yet at the same time, it would be improper to offer an account of Byatt's total literary achievement to date that gives the impression that her relatively late breakthrough came from nowhere or was pure accident. Offering, as it attempts to, a sense of continuum and totality,

3

this study must, as its first task, therefore try to characterize Byatt's unusual gifts. It may be helpful to begin with an anecdote she herself tells. At some time in the mid-1960s, between the publication of *Shadow of a Sun* (1964) and *The Game* (1967), Byatt encountered Charles Davy's *Words in the Mind* (1965). This erudite study of the language of poetry in English and French contains a chapter, 'A Game of Chess', that seems to have touched something deep in Byatt's own creative imagination.[1]

In 'A Game of Chess' Davy recalls a series of episodes in his final year at school, in which he discussed with the school chess champion the relationship between conscious thought and intuition in making the best moves at chess. After some initial resistance, the 18-year-old champion, 'J.', admitted that he visualized the various chess pieces 'as though they had lashing tails', the size and dynamics of the tail in question corresponding to the moves permitted to each piece. To simplify a rather complex analysis, Davy noted that, in visualizing the game in this way, J. was able to lose sight of the board and its pieces entirely.

Experimenting further, Davy and some friends then presented J. with two alternative solutions to a particular problem, one of which was 'very strong and solid'; the other – ostensibly absurd – was nevertheless preferred by J. because it appealed so compellingly to J.'s aesthetic sense that (though 'equally strong but not so massive' in Davy's words) it had an arresting 'fragility' about it. The absurdity of the move J. chose became evident as he proceeded with his fragile, 'fine-drawn' pattern, and that pattern turned to ruins. Davy's experiments ended abruptly when on one occasion J., playing in his customary way, physically collapsed. He then:

> struggled up immediately, crying 'I see the move', and reached for the board to make it (it was the right master move), but when he realised what had happened, the experience was a shock; it unnerved him. So much so that for a long time he refused not only to play chess but even to look at a chess position; he was afraid it might entrance him against his will.[2]

To give Davy due credit, he does wonder whether the entire series of episodes was a fraud, but his conclusion that it was not is really beside the point.

4

That point is that we will not come to terms with A. S. Byatt's fictional imagination unless we are prepared to make a considerable act of surrender. The anecdote of the chess-player J. – a clear avatar of the Marcus Potter who tries to explain his preternatural gifts to Lucas Simmonds in *The Virgin in the Garden* – may serve as a metaphor for what Byatt means when she says that, for her, novels are made out of language, and that she 'like[s] to write about people who think, to whom thinking is as important and exciting (and painful) as sex or eating'. In what follows we will trace A. S. Byatt's career as a writer of fiction over four decades, exploring the ways in which this intense passion for language, for the articulate expression of thought, coexists in her imaginative writing with the ways in which certain kinds of language may exercise deforming pressures on the reality they seek to describe and with a strong sense of what we may term her *poetics* of fiction: that is, her conviction that forms, patterns, and connections exist at such profound levels in strong yet fragile and finely drawn work that the writer may not even realize she has 'put' those elements into that work.

It was Iris Murdoch's moral and aesthetic conviction, pre-eminently, that the novel represents a battleground between 'real people and images', that drew A. S. Byatt as a critic to Murdoch's early work (JD 182). Although Byatt's understanding of this battleground is characteristically her own, she ardently believes (with Murdoch) that fiction is generous, tolerant, and patient: it is, in other words, unjudging. Byatt's own creative work reflects on the extent to which the writer is justified in drawing on the experiences of her own life. It asks profound questions about tradition (both literary and visual) and the individual talent. It recreates the imaginations and cultural expectations of characters and periods both similar to and very different from the writer's own – hence its interest in nineteenth-century matters such as Darwinism and communication with the spirits of the deceased; hence, too, a more general interest in the supernatural and the world of fairy tale. Byatt's work examines, often comically, the various kinds of erotic power that both art and myth can induce. It is fascinated by the interplay between fact and fiction, especially in so far as this informs the art of the literary biographer. It is prepared to grapple with complex and painful moral issues: two of these, the portrayals of 'real accident' and of marginalized middle-aged women, are discussed later in this book. Byatt has said that '[t]he novel is an agnostic form – it explores and describes; the novelist *and reader* learn more about the world along the length of the book' (emphasis added).[3] Although the effort demanded by the reader is formidably challenging, hundreds of thousands of very different kinds of reader will testify that that effort has been most handsomely repaid.

2

Detached Autonomy: Fathers, Daughters, and Sisters

A. S. Byatt has described herself as 'a very private person'. As her reservations about the biographer's art suggest, she believes that '[a]rt can only exist if the artist is private' (JD 191). All the same, it is rare to find a writer so generously candid about how the creative process works. Certain related conclusions can be drawn from this apparent paradox. Byatt herself points out that 'Iris Murdoch likes to separate her philosophy from her novels; David Lodge says that his critical and narrative selves are a schizoid pair. I have never felt such a separation, nor wanted to make such claims' (PM 1). The result is a writer who is prepared to discuss her work in such a way as to affirm no different kind of authority from that enjoyed by any perceptive and intelligent reader. Writing and reading are for Byatt points along a spectrum. Of course many writers affect candour about their work; but on closer examination such candour can be seen to represent an attempt, whether conscious or not, to direct their readers' responses towards authorized versions of that work.

Byatt is unusual in being possessed (possibly against her will) by a compulsive vulnerable intellectual honesty that some readers might consider inconvenient in a writer. She will say quite disarmingly what particular *donnée* gave rise to a particular work, or what particular effect she was trying to achieve in using a given narrative form or metaphor or symbol, and she will willingly keep her mind open to the discovery of further operations of the subconscious, discerned long after the event

7

of writing. Byatt's candour compels us to take her at her word when she says that she dislikes any kind of fictional writing that seeks to aggrandize or diminish the author, and it lends a quite exceptional authority to her conception of what is proper in any autobiographical status to which her fiction appears to lay claim.

It is important to establish this aspect of Byatt's moral and literary identity at the beginning of a chapter that examines what seem the most autobiographical aspects of her work, which are her depictions of relationships between fathers and daughters and between sisters. The relationship between a father and a daughter is central to Byatt's first novel, *The Shadow of the Sun* (as it is to the later short story 'Sugar'), and that between two sisters is central to *The Game*.

In *The Shadow of the Sun* (preference is given here to the revised title, a quotation from Raleigh, that Byatt originally wanted to use), the clearly intelligent but underachieving girl, Anna Severell, must work her way loose from the influence of a dominant father, Henry. The visionary Henry Severell, Byatt makes clear, is *not* a portrait of her own father: if anything, he is (as she wrote in 1991) 'partly simply my secret self' (*STS* x). But, if there is a writer on whom he is based, that writer is D. H. Lawrence, whom (rather like the critic F. R. Leavis) Byatt feels she 'cannot escape and cannot love' (*STS* xii). Henry is jokily described as 'look[ing] like a cross between God, Alfred Lord Tennyson, and Blake's Job' (*STS* 9). Henry as visionary is a type who will recur in Marcus Potter in the *roman fleuve*, which to date consists of *The Virgin in the Garden* (1978), *Still Life* (1985), and *Babel Tower* (1996).

Because Byatt has herself supplied an Introduction to the 1991 Vintage reissue of *The Shadow of the Sun*, and because space is limited, a few issues only will be raised briefly here. Anna's relationships, with her father and with her father's exegete Oliver Canning, who briefly becomes her lover while she is at Cambridge, are attempts to assert her autonomy. That autonomy consists primarily of the need to construct herself as a woman in a world where all the visionary myths and the exegetic privileges are male: in this respect, *The Shadow of the Sun* is an early contemporary assertion of a feminist programme that is remarkably recalcitrant to any desire whatsoever to ghettoize 'the woman's novel'.

Byatt does not shy away from the attractiveness of the prevailing male myths: the most memorable passages in the novel, inspired by the work of the painters Samuel Palmer and Vincent van Gogh, accompany one of Henry's 'attacks of vision' (*STS* 58). Henry, as though possessed, goes on a long walk that takes him *across and through* the usual routes of communication between fellow-humans. He stumbles (can we say obliviously?) through a cornfield:

> And still the light poured, heavy, and white, and hot, into the valley before him and collected, molten and seething, on the corn beneath him; he could hear it thundering into the silence; and still he had to see, so that his cone [of vision] was now an hourglass funnel, opening both ways, and the wide light all pressed and weighed in the point of intersection which was himself, and the gold figures, hieratic, with gold faces and swords of flame, walked in the sea of corn in ordered patterns, like reapers; he recognized them from before, and he knew that he had come to the end.... To see like this was to be alive ... (*STS* 80)

Such purple prose is nowhere given to Anna, but this fact can be seen as actually contributing to Anna's sense of autonomy. At a late point in the novel, Anna, wandering on to the Silver Street bridge in Cambridge after a party, feels she is about to have a vision ('She thought, this is going to be important'), but it dissolves, and she sees

> that she had not been stirred out of herself, she had been moved only as far as a secondhand reflection, in a literary manner, in Oliver's manner, on a piece of prose (secondhand, reflective prose at that) about an experience that in its real, far, unimaginable depth belonged properly to her father. She was still small, and self-contained and watching, and the possible glory was gone. (*STS* 237–8)

This is a bare, sparse language that sounds like failure, but it is to be understood in terms of Anna's beginning to exercise her own autonomy. In this sense it represents a modest triumph that, from the perspective of the 1990s, now seems fully *earned*. Anna sees things in this way not because she is a woman but because she is not a visionary. For the gender-political point to be made, what Byatt has termed the 'fate' that she herself 'feared' must be faced squarely. The task will now be to find a language proper to 'female vision, female art and thought'. With her first novel, Byatt embarked on a quest for appropriate images '(amongst others, and not without interest in the male too)' (*STS*, p. xiv). Like George Eliot, Byatt has been accused 'of not joining in' with feminism; like Eliot, too, she has in her own age produced 'powerful images of what it was like to be a woman who couldn't use what she had got' (NT 61).

Joanne V. Creighton has observed that A. S. Byatt, like her real-life sister Margaret Drabble, 'is reluctant to discuss their [sibling] relationship and anxious to minimize it as a critical concern'.[1] This attitude commands respect, not least because a reading of *The Game* as a simple *roman à clef* about two ambitious sisters who write debases the novel and proffers an allegorical perspective that the text itself simply cannot sustain. It is more fruitful to consider Julia and Cassandra Corbett as representing two split facets of the creative writer's imagination. Neither necessarily exerts moral superiority over the other; certainly neither is absolutely 'right'. It is true that Julia lies and steals, but Cassandra's pathological honesty has a dangerously vindictive streak to it.

Almost imperceptibly we realize we are being drawn into a world that is intense, unstable, and frightening. The childhood Game that Cassandra and Julia have evolved calls up a lost paradise, and is at this level explicitly reminiscent of the Brontë children's Angria creations. Cassandra's control over the childhood Game is undermined by Julia's pragmatism: 'For years [Julia] had kept secret the fact that the drawer which held Cassandra's journal could be worked open with the key of her mother's sewing-machine. Indeed, she did not know now whether Cassandra had known this' (*G.* 46). In this way, the sisters come to possess each other. *The Game*, in fact, adumbrates *Possession*, just as does *The Shadow of a Sun*.

In *The Game* what may be considered normal sibling rivalry soon modulates into a psychopathological complexity that is reflected in the tensely knotted difficult narrative sequence recalling an episode in which Julia, aged 16, had won a short-story competition in a national children's magazine. The 18-year-old Cassandra 'knew immediately what had happened. She thought she had always known it would happen, and had pushed it out of her mind' (*G.* 70).

What *has* happened is only then revealed: Julia has appropriated and simplified Cassandra's version of a story that 'concerned Sir Lancelot, benighted in the forest, bludgeoned into temptation by four queens'. Cassandra's essay, submitted three years earlier as a school exercise, had been criticized for being over-imaginative, but now Cassandra feels 'outrage':

> She could not accuse Julia of simple theft – the story was, or had been, common property. And Julia's story, although it abounded in similarities of phrasing and passages of description, was in many ways better than her own lumpy version: it was more controlled and had an element of amused irony that was intensified by the drawings – rather *art nouveau* – which accompanied it. (G. 70–71)

In interview, Byatt has said that 'one of the reasons for [her] dislike of the women's fiction' written by Julia is that 'it's self-indulgent creation, the "waste fertility" with which Comus tempts the Lady in Milton's *Comus*, a denial of real fertility and real freedom' (JD 186).

Earlier a family row in front of Cassandra has provoked from Julia's disillusioned adolescent daughter Deborah the acerbic observation: 'That . . . will be a hundred guineas from the New Yorker when it's written up. She always writes up rows' (G. 60). The insouciance profoundly shocks Cassandra, who comes during the course of *The Game* to realize, as does Julia, that (as Olga Kenyon puts it) their childhood inventions have '[fed] the imagination to a point where neither [sister] can mature nor free herself of awareness of the other'.[2] Cassandra, the amateur writer of a journal, needs to speak: Julia, the professional best-selling novelist who writes for money, needs to be heard. Whereas Cassandra writes things down, Julia writes them up. Byatt herself has remarked that 'Cassandra sees writing as artifice and Julia sees writing as natural, and Cassandra is the better writer' (NT 66). Jane Campbell augments this observation: 'By including the novelist in her novel – as Juliet did not in hers – Byatt takes account of the moral problems of art and shows herself to be a better novelist than Julia'.[3]

The two sisters come to seem, each in her own way, hideously conjoined. (In *Babel Tower* Frederica Potter and John Ottokar will discuss this kind of feeling, about partner and identical twin sibling, respectively.) Conjunction is recapitulated in Byatt's work in the relationship between father and daughter. In the autobiographical short story 'Sugar', the narrator remarks that her father

> had often said . . . that a man's children are his true and only immortality. As a girl I had been made uncomfortable by that idea. I craved separation. 'Each man is an island' was my version of a delightful if melancholy truth. I was like Auden's version of Prospero's rejecting brother, Antonio, 'By choice myself alone'. (*SOS* 232)

Many of Byatt's readers may find it hard to resist making further connections, such as that the fear of being conjoined may represent a subconscious memory of the image of the snake that has swallowed the toad in Virginia Woolf's *Between the Acts* (1941) and is choked ('Dead? No . . . The snake was unable to swallow, the toad was unable to die. A spasm made the ribs contract; blood oozed. It was birth the wrong way round – a monstrous inversion').[4] Or they may find an equally subconscious recall of *Paradise Lost*, bk 10, in which Satan, returning triumphantly to Hell after seducing first Eve then Adam, undergoes a genuinely serpentine metamorphosis:

> His visage drawn he felt to sharp and spare,
> His arms clung to his ribs, his legs entwining
> Each other, till supplanted down he fell,
> A monstrous serpent on his belly prone,
> Reluctant, but in vain . . .

> (10 511–15)

This episode in turn parodically Christianizes the story of Cadmus as told by Ovid in *Metamorphoses* 4. Pressed by Juliet Dusinberre in interview as to whether the snake (also 'Coleridge's symbol of the imagination forever uncoiling') might additionally stand for 'the source of wisdom and art, the image for creativity', Byatt conceded that: 'The serpent is both sex and destruction, and imagination and preservation, and these two are curiously and intimately combined' (JD 193).

Connections such as these are attractive because they indicate the complexity of the snake imagery in *The Game*, a complexity the text and its characters seem to encourage – all the characters, that is, except one: the professional herpetologist Simon Moffitt, with whom the snakes are primarily associated. Prior to the novel's action Simon has been loved by Cassandra and lost to Julia. (Julia has gone on to marry the Norwegian Quaker Thor Eskelund, and is carrying on a half-hearted affair with the TV producer Ivan Rostrevor.) For Simon, the snakes are snakes first: they are not weighed down with accretive myths such as those mentioned above (*G.* 161). Simon tries unavailingly to hold on to his autonomy: in an unused take for the TV transmission of *The Lively Arts* he loses his temper in front of Julia and Ivan: ' "You can make anything of me," said Simon, "as you can make anything of snakes. But I don't like it. I didn't come here to be psychoanalysed. I came here to discuss my work. *My* work . . ." ' (*G.* 162).

Simon is still traumatized by an event in which his cameraman Antony has been stripped to the bone by pirhanas in front of Simon's eyes. There are no myths there. But Simon's voice is unheard by the text, its characters – and the ingenious reader. In the connivance that excludes Simon, not only do Simon's snakes recall the literary allusions of inseparability mentioned above, they also and additionally (Byatt's uses of tradition are never exclusive) recall Medusa (a figure who will return in *The Matisse Stories*). Ovid's *Metamorphoses* 4 ends with the story of Perseus slaying Medusa, avoiding her mortal gaze by using her reflection in the polished bronze shield: the idea of inseparability is enhanced by the idea of both the mirror and the severing of the Medusa head as (respectively) an instrument for, and the means of, survival. Byatt shares Iris Murdoch's assertion that, for Jean-Paul Sartre (about whom Murdoch published a short book in 1953), 'the Medusa's snakes represent . . . our fear of being watched, overlooked' (*IC* 173).

Julia's public profile and her final fatal writing up of Simon and Cassandra in her novel *A Sense of Glory* are her response to this fear of being watched. It is Cassandra to whom Julia's version of this fear proves fatal. Cassandra, who has abandoned her Quaker upbringing for a nostalgic Anglo-Catholicism, is perceived by her parish priest, Fr Gerald Rowell, as heading towards some kind of nervous breakdown. He fails adequately to intervene, and Cassandra's final Journal entry reads: 'There is nowhere I shall not drag this grotesque shadow, our joint creature. I can choose, at least, to put out the light that throws it. I want no more reflections', (*G.* 230). Cassandra can no longer live without reference to Julia's fictional version of herself. Olga Kenyon has related Cassandra's suicide (her successful bid for detached autonomy) to the way in which George Eliot, whose *Mill on the Floss* Byatt edited for Penguin, has Maggie Tulliver drown at the end of that novel.[5] All the same, Byatt still appears to feel that Eliot's disposal of Maggie is inappropriate. Writing in 1980, Byatt complained:

> drowning *with her brother* was not (and I must say is not) a fate for Maggie Tulliver that leaves one with any feeling of having really come to the end – tragic, passionate, despondent – of the complexities of cross, clever, ferocious Maggie. The author drowned the heroine for dramatic reasons ... (*PM* 72).

This complaint sheds supporting light on the death of Cassandra as an act of detachment from the constraints of being conjoined. That death is the opposite of 'dramatic': it is essential, and it is real.

3

Erotic Power, Art, and Myth

In Iris Murdoch's novel *The Black Prince* (1973), the failed 58-year-old writer Bradley Pearson falls in love with Julian. This adolescent girl, named after the medieval visionary Dame Julian of Norwich, is the daughter of his friend and rival, the prolific Arnold Baffin. Bradley's experience stimulates, as a kind of swansong, the work we read as *The Black Prince*. The circumstances surrounding that experience are worth closer examination. A. S. Byatt has written perceptively of both. According to Byatt, 'the love of an old man for a girl is something which Bradley, from the outside, sees as "ugly and pathetic" ' (*DF* 269). Once it has overtaken him himself, however, '[Bradley's] passion for Julian (ambiguously male and female as she is) converts all [the] negatives to positives in the context of the passion itself' (*DF* 270). Bradley is overtaken by what he describes as 'absolute charm'. Murdoch sees such 'charm' as dangerous, and Byatt clearly subscribes to this view. Although every aspect of human activity and indeed existence that had previously disgusted Bradley now appears beautiful, Byatt reminds us that Murdoch 'has several times spoken of the human tendency to "deform" reality by seeing it through egocentric fantasy' (*DF* 270). The vehicle for this fantasy is art itself.

Among many striking instances in Murdoch's work of the human tendency to 'deform' reality by seeing it through the egocentric fantasies that art provides are two that occur in *The Black Prince* itself. They shed engrossing light on certain facets of Byatt's own gifts. Somewhere between the beginning and the end of a private 'tutorial' on *Hamlet*, Bradley discovers that he has fallen in love with Julian. If at the time that moment is not guessed at, it becomes evident later when, having 'eloped' with Bradley, Julian dresses up as Hamlet for a joke, provoking a violent sexual assault by Bradley that frightens Julian because it is so completely at variance with the couple's previous unsuccessful attempts at love-making. The turning-point during the tutorial is seen in retrospect to have been Julian's admission that she had once played Hamlet in a school production. Murdoch's title takes on increasing richness: Byatt points out that the Black Prince

> is an object of love and terror, [he] is a composite god-demon in the novel; he is Apollo, the god of light and art, but also the cruel god, who punished the faun, Marsyas [Ovid, *Metamorphoses* 6], by flaying him for daring to compete with him as an artist. He is Shakespeare and Hamlet, he is Love and Death, and Art. (*DF* 271)

Of all Byatt's novels to date, it is *The Virgin in the Garden* that engages most fully with the erotic power exercised both by the work of art and by the mythic power of art. Byatt is fascinated by Murdoch's belief, itself derived from Freud and Plato, that art (and by implication art as myth) acts iconically between the artist and what Freud terms the 'client'. Art and myth have the unique power of softening the egotistical character of daydream, thus overcoming the repulsion that would be felt by human beings for each other if their true fantasy lives could be known for what they really are. The mistrust felt by Plato in particular is grounded in his belief that the erotic power of art and myth tricks the human soul into lowering its guard: Eros is deceptive, mischievous, a trickster.

In *The Virgin in the Garden* this theme is explored centrally and comically in the explicitly sexualized and frequently farcical goings-on that accompany rehearsals and performance of Alexander Wedderburn's verse drama *Astraea*. Anyone who has been involved in amateur dramatics will recognize these obscure and powerful forces, which are described with exactitude by Olga Kenyon.[1] In conversation with Ignês Sodré Byatt has challengingly spoken of their role in the plotting of Jane Austen's *Mansfield Park* and the *Lovers' Vows* theatricals in that novel (*IC* 24–31). At various levels, as Byatt and Sodré agree, use of the play can 'enrich' the novel. There is also, in *The Virgin in the Garden*, a serious organic subplot involving the power of Eros in the lives of Daniel Orton and Stephanie Potter; this subplot is illustrated during a scene on the beach at Filey on the North Yorkshire coast, when Daniel and Stephanie are, it could be argued, 'taken over' by Eros the trickster under his guise as Venus Anadyomene. What is particularly interesting about this scene in Byatt's artistic development is how the Anadyomene myth is later reviewed and restated with reference to Filey within the context of the gender politics of *Possession*.

It must be understood that Byatt's understanding of realism differs quite fundamentally from Murdoch's. Murdoch's novels are set in a quasi-realistic environment that many readers think of as 'Murdochland'. This 'omniverse' is geographically distinct, remote from what most contemporary readers would think of as the infrastructural realities of everyday life (TV and word processors are largely banished from its terms of reference), frequently moneyed and high-bourgeois, and possessed of a system of sexual morals that may be thought to transgress normative experience. In her ongoing *roman fleuve* Byatt, in contrast, meshes a wealth of detailed celebratory descriptions (of food and arrangements of flowers; of authentic and at the same time absurd sex) with a frankly self-conscious reference to literary tradition and colour symbolism as these present themselves in the quotidian lives of a highly intellectual Yorkshire family and those with whom they have to do. As Juliet Dusinberre has usefully shown, *The Virgin in the Garden* is both realistic and experimental simultaneously.[2]

These various elements combine to form an admission of the impossibility of writing without in some way having recourse to the figurative associations that inevitably accrete around words. It is certainly possible to read Byatt's novels as complex social realism, as, for instance, D. J. Taylor tends to (the germ of *The Virgin in the Garden* appears to be Byatt's announced conviction that one *could* still write a novel with the provincial reach of *Middlemarch* in the late twentieth century), but her work is enriched beyond measure when the reader surrenders to its status as fiction about post-war English society that is unconditionally embedded in the cultural background designating that society. Frederica Potter in particular is articulately committed to the idea that the culture of which she is a part is, like her own growing experience, 'laminated': layered or cumulative (*VG* 274–5). This is an idea she will need urgently to develop in *Babel Tower*. Of the figurative potential that background offers, Byatt herself has written:

> Below the metaphoric patterning of the text there runs a colour-patterning – red for blood, white for stone, green for grass. I should say that this is made explicit and is also the patterning of the metaphoric structure of the verse-drama in the play. (*PM* 10)

It should not therefore seem surprising that the schoolmaster Alexander Wedderburn, a writer convinced in 1953 of the viability of the verse drama, that was self-consciously revived in the mid-twentieth century by T. S. Eliot and Christopher Fry, should attempt the form himself. Wedderburn is also heir to Eliot's belief (shared in 1953 by Byatt *in propria persona*) in the full recuperability of sixteenth- and seventeenth-century English literature, in other words to belief in 'Eliot's elegant fiction of the undissociated sensibility, in which Donne felt his thought as immediately as the odour of a rose' (*PM* 2). (Byatt, unlike Wedderburn, will later quarrel with Eliot's restriction of this apprehension to the pre-Restoration poets when she argues, in 1990, that Tennyson and Browning 'of course, and in fact, do exactly the same, as an examination of the yew trees in *In Memoriam*, or of "Karshish", will demonstrate', and she sees her own earlier belief in Eliot's the dissociation of sensibility as serving her as a 'lost paradise' (*PM* 2).) In *The Virgin in the Garden* Wedderburn is thus led to connect the reigns of the two Elizabeths (1558–1603 and 1952 onwards). Yet he remains suspicious of deutero-Elizabethan establishment propaganda. He is offended by the way in which the BBC's TV coverage of the 1953 Coronation presented 'Richard Dimbleby [choosing] to emphasise his encomium of Elizabeth II with sharp disparagement of Elizabeth I'. Here are the words of the BBC transcript, incorporated into Byatt's text:

> 'By contrast, the first Elizabeth, with the lusty imperious Henry VIII as her father and the scheming Anne Boleyn for mother, was not perhaps without some qualifications for the title "the daughter of the devil" which the Spanish ambassador bestowed upon her. In mitigation she could offer evidence of a childhood that would make most of the twentieth-century's broken homes to which young criminals' delinquencies are so often attributed seem highly respectable.

This grim childhood fostered the development of her wiles and cunning . . .' (*VG* 321)

Evidence of the complexity of Wedderburn's vision – we are told that his feelings towards the second Elizabeth '[as] cried up by Dimbleby were lukewarm at best' (*VG* 321) – is supplied by an episode in his own verse drama *Astraea* that recurs several times in the plot of *The Virgin in the Garden*. It recurs precisely because of the intensity of the effort of rehearsal that goes into it and the erotic force with which it is charged. It provokes prurient interest among the other actors in *Astraea*, and indeed other characters in *The Virgin in the Garden*. This provocation is an expression of the deep ambivalence of Wedderburn's own presence as an erotic icon (at least three women are in love with him, and the narrator herself is not unmoved by his physical grace and beauty – yet his sexuality seems recalcitrant to satisfactory definition). It is also a telling example of the ways in which Eros exerts his dangerous and mischievous powers on a group of people, the best part of whose souls' guard (as Plato might have said) is lowered as they succumb to the illusory nature of art and myth.

Frederica is cast as the youthful Princess Elizabeth, daughter of her father's second wife Anne Boleyn. Recent scholarship has examined the ménage in which Elizabeth lived in the late 1540s – that is, in the household of Elizabeth's stepfather Thomas Seymour (brother of her father's third wife and guardian of her own half-brother, the sickly and youthful Edward VI) and Seymour's wife Katherine Parr, who had been widowed (not for the first time) on the death of Elizabeth's father, whose sixth wife she had been. The persistent anecdotes of cavortings among Seymour, Parr, and the young Princess have been contextualized by recent scholarship into theoretical discussions of early modern sexuality. It has been asked whether these anecdotal cavortings do not form a kind of incest. The anecdotes themselves find their way prominently into Wedderburn's play. At one point the rehearsal is not going well: Alexander suggests that Frederica wear a 'real long skirt'. A number of actors from the next scene wander in:

> This time the scene went better. Wrath, Alexander's touch, a half-glimpse of Jenny's bare brown shoulder and newly-washed hair

brought considerable life to Frederica's riddling invitations and rebuffs. The petticoats gave her something to do with her redundant hands. Joanne Plummer of her own accord laid a restraining hand on the girl's scrawny shoulder, and Frederica winced royally and convincingly, addressing herself in mock rebuke to the empty air somewhere between Sid Gorman and Alexander Wedderburn. 'I am not used to be so used,' she said, and the voice had at last the combination of dry impatience and involuntary lewdness that had kindled Lodge at the auditions. Gorman was provoked to genuine aggression; he brought the girl down, rather heavily, with a kind of rugger tackle, and Joanne Plummer, excited by the shears which she brandished above her head began to laugh and snip and laugh and snip with real hysteria, waving the scissors in the air between slashes, whilst Gorman tore with some deliberation at the paper between Frederica's legs. Shreds and floating scraps of white paper, like fallen petals, settled on pond and lawn: Frederica wriggled free, clutching her own skirt against her crotch and chanting, rudely, nervously, cleverly as Alexander had intended, the old woman's cry from the ancient ballad. 'Lawks a' mussy on me, this is none of I.' The audience applauded. (VG 380–1)

It is tempting to identify Frederica with Elizabeth (she is after all the virgin in the garden). The scenario offers other kinds of potential identification. It disturbingly reverberates against Hamlet's 'uncle-father' and 'aunt-mother'. Seymour fulfils a role that is offered to Alexander Wedderburn, Matthew Crowe, and Edmund Wilkie in turn. Katherine Parr seems to stand in for the absent Shakespearian mother. In other words, the casting, which is itself a kind of metaphor, works on several levels simultaneously, just as do the other metaphors in Byatt's text (and rather more complexly than do the castings of Lovers' Vows in Mansfield Park).

Frederica's acting is counterpointed by that of her younger brother Marcus, whose major achievement in life so far has been to play 'a chilling and extraordinary Ophelia' (VG 29). But Marcus's role in The Virgin in the Garden is primarily an exploration of his vulnerable psyche in partnership with the schoolmaster Lucas Simmonds and the latter's dotty metaphysics. This does involve erotic forces, but characteristically the relationship between the two is no stereotypical seduction of pupil by teacher – nor, indeed, vice versa. Juliet Dusinberre perceptively observes that Alexander, who is (like so many of

Byatt's characters) a meticulous reader of the written word, also resembles many of them in being poor observers of 'lived' reality. As a result he *is* reduced to seeing the affair as a stereotype.[3] We are faced (as we are repeatedly faced in Byatt's fiction) with the dismaying possibility that ingenious readers can be blind to what is real.

A more interesting counterpoint is formed by Stephanie, and specifically by the development of her relationship with the comparatively unlettered Daniel. On his first visit to the Potter household Daniel is truculently challenged by Stephanie's puritan atheist father Bill (a kind of F. R. Leavis figure): 'There is more truth in *King Lear* as far as I know than in all the gospels put together. I want people to have life and have it abundantly, Mr Orton' (*VG* 46). Daniel is dignified in rebuke: 'I've not read *King Lear*. It wasn't set for Higher when I did it. I'll repair the omission.' (*VG* 47). Later, in *Babel Tower*, we will see that he is able to echo Lear on watching his concussed daughter Mary regain consciousness: 'Look there – look at her lips' (*BT* 47). But in *The Virgin in the Garden* Daniel's reparation of the omission already reveals a mixture of motives that again illuminate the mysterious interactions of Art and Eros:

> As he came to the end [of *King Lear*] he realised he had learned something about pain. His body was strained and stiff. He felt stirred and apprehensive – something to do with the reading, more with Stephanie Potter. . . . Whilst her father preached to him, he had imagined, with extraordinary clarity, that he might lean forward and take hold of her round lazy ankle and grip, grip till the bones shifted. (*VG* 71)

(Lucas Simmonds's final manifestation of insanity before being institutionalized recalls Lear, bare and forked, garlanded with flowers.) Here, Daniel's reading of *King Lear* anticipates the extraordinary chapter, entitled 'Anadyomene', in which Daniel takes Stephanie to visit the beach at Filey.

Whatever it is that happens to Daniel and Stephanie at Filey, they are shown undergoing a mystical experience that apparently changes their lives forever: that experience may be defined (in a comparable way to that in which the art-object *Hamlet* acts on Bradley Pearson and Julian Baffin) as the entry of the dark god Eros into their lives. Daniel and Stephanie manage to clamber onto the Brigg:

21

[Stephanie] stood there as though mesmerised by the water, her mouth open slightly, smiling secretly, while the wind rippled on in her wet hair and clothes. The sun was so bright now [Daniel] could hardly see her. A smaller wave failed to hurl itself as high as they were. She again said something he could not hear. . . . 'Come on,' she said. She began to go out along the rocks, very fast, holding her arms wide to balance herself, half-running, half-striding. He went after her. Another tall wave bowed, jarred, cracked and whispered at her feet. She turned to him a face he had never seen, blindly smiling, wild, white and wet. As she set off again, another wave rose, Daniel seized her, the drenching waters descended, and Daniel took hold of her hair and body. He kissed her. There was a mixture of salt and cold and heat and unbalance. She kissed him back. She kissed him so certainly that they both staggered and Daniel could only right them by tugging her hair and shoving with his knees. This caused her to be pliant and docile, who had been straining and flying. (*VG* 235–6)

What claims for the authenticity of this experience are being made? Is this 'the real thing' or merely another collusion between Eros the trickster and (in this case) the artistry of myth? The question seems to resist any answer more direct than citation from *Possession*. In that novel Filey can do no more for the acquisitive Mortimer Cropper than spawn illicit biographical speculation about Randolph Henry Ash and Ash alone. Yet Filey, it so transpires, is one of several sites visited by Ash and Christabel LaMotte (as the teasingly omniscient narrator reveals), as it is later to be visited by the literary detectives Roland and Maud. Filey clearly occupies a special place at many levels of *Possession*. But it does not reveal itself as working on the erotic imaginations of *Possession*'s characters as it does on those of Daniel and Stephanie. The most remarkable reference to the location occurs in a passage of scholarship authored by Leonora Stern:

'And what surfaces of the earth do we women choose to celebrate, who have appeared typically in phallocentric texts as a penetrable hole, inviting or abhorrent, surrounded by, fringed with – something? Women writers and painters are seen to have created their own significantly evasive landscapes, with features which deceive or elude the penetrating gaze, tactile landscapes which do not privilege the dominant stare. The heroine takes pleasure in a world which is both bare and not [b]ushy, which has small hillocks and rises, with tufts of scrub and gently prominent rocky parts which disguise sloping declivities, hidden clefts, not one but a multitude of hidden holes and openings through which life-giving waters bubble and enter reciprocally. ... I myself believe that the pleasure of the fall of waves on the shores is to be added to this delight, their regular breaking bearing a profound relation to the successive shivering delights of the female orgasm. There is a marine and salty wave-water to be figured which is not, as Venus Anadyomene was, put together out of the crud of male semen scattered on the deep at the moment of the emasculation of Father Time by his Oedipal son. Such pleasure in the shapeless yet patterned succession of waters, in the formless yet formed sequence of waves on the shore, is essentially present in the art of Virginia Woolf and the form of her sentences, her utterance, themselves. I can only marvel at the instinctive delicacy and sensitivity of those female companions of Charlotte Brontë who turned aside when she first came face to face with the power of the sea at Filey, and waited peacefully until, her body trembling, her face flushed, her eyes wet, she was able to rejoin her companions and walk on with them.' (P. 244)

Here, it would seem, Leonora has managed to describe the actions of artistic myth in such a way as to suggest how the egocentric and deforming fantasy powers of Eros might after all be resisted within a work of art. Yet the description remains Leonora's, and needs to be juxtaposed (for instance) with Sabine de Kercoz's account of how she took a clearly disturbed Christabel LaMotte to the bay at Fouesnant in Brittany, where the two women

listened to the breakers and the gulls crying, quite still, quite still. Her eyes were closed when I came up with her, and with every breaker her brows creased in a little frown. I had the fanciful idea that they were beating on her skull like blows, and that she was *enduring* the sound, for reasons of her own. I went away again – I have never met anyone who so gave the impression that normal acts of friendliness are a deadly intrusion. (P. 347)

Given Byatt's reservations about how feminist reading can go behind the artefact, invading it and destroying the conditions that create art (JD 191), we must remain content with the Chinese-box possibility that Byatt is using Leonora's passage ironically, more as a revelation to us of her scholarly psyche than incontestably as an affirmation of Byatt's own sense of concord with Leonora's conception of the waves.

4

The Private Life

As is now well known to its readers, *Possession* (in A. S. Byatt's account) began life as its title as early as 1974, some sixteen years before its publication. In terms of content *Possession* was apparently inspired by Byatt's realization, while researching in the British Library her 1970 study that was reissued in 1989 as *Unruly Times*, that the Coleridge scholar Kathleen Coburn, also to be seen working there, 'can't have had a thought for the last thirty years that isn't in some sense his thought ... everything I know about his thought has been put together for me by her' (EW 78–9).

And, as Byatt put it to Nicolas Tredell:

> it came to me that possession worked both ways – she thought Coleridge's thoughts and his thoughts were entirely mediated by her. Then much later I got the ideas of the spiritualist mediums, possession in that sense, and sexual possession, if you had two poets rather than one, and economic possession. (NT 58)

It was Robert Browning rather than Coleridge who formed the male poetic inspiration for Randolph Henry Ash in *Possession*. Indeed the very beginning of the narrative of *Possession* itself alludes to that of Browning's *The Ring and the Book*. *Possession* begins with Roland Michell's discovery of a draft of the inception of a hitherto undiscovered correspondence between Ash and Christabel LaMotte. But it is what the draft letters are found *in* that should command our attention:

> The book was thick and black and covered with dust. Its boards were bowed and creaking; it had been maltreated in its own time. Its spine was missing, or rather protruded from amongst the leaves like a bulky marker. It was bandaged about and about with dirty white tape, tied in a neat bow. (P. 1)

This opening rather uncannily echoes the first Book of *The Ring and the Book*, which, together with its last, are the only ones in this extraordinary poem to be uttered in Browning's own voice:

> Do you see this square old yellow Book, I toss
> I'the air, and catch again, and twirl about
> By the crumpled vellum covers, – pure crude fact
> Secreted from man's life when hearts beat hard,
> And brains, high-blooded, ticked two centuries since?
> Examine it yourselves! I found this book,
> Gave a *lira* for it, eightpence English just . . .

(I. 33–39)

In propria persona Browning goes on to relate that he made his find in a Florentine market and paid what he was asked for it; Roland, in contrast, pilfers Ash's drafts and xeroxes them. Jean-Louis Chevalier sensitively relates Roland's act to the epigraph to the first chapter of *Possession*, from the fictional Ash's *The Garden of Proserpina* (1861), a passage repeated at greater length as the epigraph to the twenty-sixth chapter:

> Until the tricksy hero Herakles
> Came to his dispossession and the theft.

Roland's act has mythic as well as literary antecedents;[1] reference to Herakles' role in the Persephone/Proserpine abduction myth is a wonderfully judged piece of ironic intertextuality. Herakles' rescue of Alcestis from Hades (Thanatos or Death) inverts Pluto's abduction of Persephone, who (though also rescued, by Demeter at Zeus' behest) must nevertheless remain in Hades for half of each year. Byatt has repeatedly spoken of the attractive power that the Persephone myth exerts on her imagination (see, for instance, NT 71). Herakles' intervention is thus benevolent (if 'tricksy'), and it beautifully complements (and ethically tempers) Roland's act. It is that act that unleashes the discovery of the events that the scholarly biographers attempt (not, of course, wholly successfully) to trace. In contrast, Browning uses *his* find – a mishmash of printed text and hand-written commentary he feels compelled to make sense of – to construct, through his characteristic virtuoso ventriloquy, a palimpsest in which ten out of the twelve books are devoted to

25

various voices' accounts of the same events. Those events are a squalid tale of arranged marriage and murder in Rome in 1698.

Byatt has reflected on Browning's insistence on how 'pure crude fact' is made into fiction in *The Ring and the Book* (*PM* 43–51): having made the outcome of his story clear before letting any of his voices speak, Browning asks:

> Is fiction which makes fact alive, fact too?
> The somehow may be thishow.

(I. 706–7)

The passage will be familiar also as the epigraph to 'Precipice-Encurled', except that Byatt adds a comma after 'fiction': Jane Campbell has pointed out that, by 'adding the comma where Browning did not use one, [Byatt] suggests that fiction-making is inevitable whenever the imagination is at work on the facts'.[2]

Roland's find, too, assumes the status of 'pure crude fact', but it has been appropriated out of another text that is 'known': it is the London Library's copy of Jules Michelet's Vico that had belonged to Ash. In this way (one of a variety of ways), Byatt is able to realize her conviction that the twentieth-century scholars who are 'working on' the nineteenth-century originals are somehow less 'real' than the originals. The twentieth-century scholars' construction of the Ash–LaMotte relationship is predicated on chance (as was Browning's discovery of the 'square old yellow Book'), but what the twentieth-century scholars then embark on is a series of appropriations that they attempt (unavailingly as it turns out) to *control*, to possess spiritualistically, economically, sexually. Browning, in contrast, lets the various protagonists speak for themselves, which they do (frequently contradicting each others' accounts), and he withholds judgement at the end. Some of the actions of Byatt's characters are (figuratively speaking) as reprehensible as those of Browning's. Even so, Byatt has realized that it is not possible to create, in the late twentieth century, the kind of novel that she believes to be lurking behind Browning's poem.

The assumption that R. H. Ash in *Possession* 'stands for' Robert Browning needs a brief preliminary examination. The earlier story 'Precipice-Encurled' is constructed around Byatt's response to an event that actually occurred in historical fact and is recorded in a letter of Browning's to an American lady living in Venice, Mrs Kay Bronson: in the summer of 1882 Browning and his sister Sarianna (who had become his companion after Elizabeth Barrett Browning's death in 1861) cancelled a visit to the Cholmondely family on the island of Ischia because a Miss Wade, a young guest of the Cholmondely household, had fallen to her death from a ledge while sketching the sunset.[3] Mrs Bronson was (as it also happens) a close friend of Henry James. Byatt has made clear that she made no attempt to research the event itself. Instead, as she has written, she found herself angered at the twentieth-century scholarly editor of the Browning–Bronson correspondence, Michael Meredith, who exists in fact and may (or may not) be the unnamed scholar mentioned in Byatt's story. In his anxiety to speculate on the blossoming of some kind of relationship between Browning and Mrs Bronson, Meredith relegates a young life, with all its potential, to a footnote. Of Meredith's 1985 edition of the corres- pondence Byatt has remarked: 'J'ai alors pensé: «Toute une jeune existence, et la terreur dans sa totalité, incidemment réduites à une note en bas de page.»' (*Fdj* 87).

This anger seems to lie behind the curious blending of fact and fiction in 'Precipice-Encurled'. The Cholmondelys have become the Fishwicks, Ischia the Apennines, and Miss Wade is fictionally reconstructed, in all her particularity, as a young male artist, Joshua Riddell. Jane Campbell suggests that 'we may recognize a feminist subtext that plays with sexual stereotypes',[4] and she has painstakingly disentangled fact from fiction in Byatt's story:

> The young painter and the old poet, the reader is made to feel, would have understood each other: they share a passion for accur- acy about the most minute and insignificant details of the human and natural worlds. The plot thus embodies one of Browning's favorite themes, opportunity missed. This narrative itself is enclosed in, and encloses, two more stories on the same theme – stories of unfulfilled love.[5]

As Campbell convincingly demonstrates, 'Precipice-Encurled' is richly intertextual. One striking element for present purposes is the plethora of quotations from and allusions to one of Henry James's stranger and less-known stories, 'The Private Life' (1891). James seems to have written this in tribute to Browning, who had died in 1889. 'The Private Life' is a benign ghost story with none of the terror of 'The Turn of the Screw'. Its unnamed narrator is staying with a group of Jamesian high society at a hotel in the Alps. Among the group is a playwright, Clare Vawtrey, who appears incapable of producing any drama for the group's delectation, and in particular for an actress named Blanche Adney. Spurred on by Blanche, the narrator discovers, however, that Vawtrey has a double, who sits in Vawtrey's hotel room, writing plays in the dark. Conversely, Blanche has discovered that another hotel guest, Lord Mellifont, physically disappears when he is not the centre of the social transactions in James's tale, a discovery the narrator also comes to share. The purpose of the story seems to have been James's desire to depict Browning (whom he greatly admired) as a man whose public life was completely at odds with his private life. '[B]luff and chatty, urgently affectionate and hortatory' in public, as Byatt puts it, Browning is completely transformed in the ventriloquist through whom his 'men and women' speak:

> Browning the animator is altogether more complex, wise and fierce, calculating and inspired, passionate and intelligent, exactly and sharply judging and endlessly, imaginatively curious about all sorts of small and obscene, trivial and terrible human desires and self-deceptions. (*PM* 29)

It is clear that Byatt's disconcerting play with fact and fiction in 'Precipice-Encurled' forms some kind of preparation for *Possession*, since both works in their very different ways show a strong dislike of biographical (mis-)appropriation. 'Precipice-Encurled', with its gestures towards James's 'The Private Life', casts revealing light on the contrast between the Ash and LaMotte (and indeed all the nineteenth-century characters) who are constructed by the biographical imaginations of the twentieth-century scholars, as opposed to such characters as they exist in the free imaginative space created for them by the novelist. Ash is *conscribed* in various ways by the twentieth-century scholars: for instance, by Mortimer Cropper in what is almost at times sexual or fetishistic fantasy, or by James Blackadder out of a sense of lack of fulfilment (that he had failed to defend Ash in one of F. R. Leavis's undergraduate seminars). LaMotte is analogously conscribed, with varying degrees of intensity, as a proto-feminist who suits the programmes of Maud Bailey or Leonora Stern.

It is this insight that allows Byatt's extraordinary creative play, as omniscient narrator, with *all* her characters. Not only can the narrator create as much imaginative space as she likes; she can use that space to mock the pretensions of those scholars who, believing they have captured the 'real' Ash or LaMotte, have simply projected their own fantasies onto those characters. The scholars are unable to 'imagine characters'; as Byatt saw, quoting Iris Murdoch's famous essay 'Against Dryness' (1961) in *Degrees of Freedom*, 'we have [in contrast to the nineteenth-century titans], as [Murdoch] sees it, "been left with far too shallow and flimsy an idea of human personality"' (*DF* 4). The biographical work of Cropper, Blackadder, Bailey, and Leonora, in a variety of ways, shows this. All they can do is shed evanescent glimpses on the public lives of Ash and LaMotte. The novelist, the omniscient narrator, enjoys much greater privilege and freedom: she can show the limitations of constructions of the public life, and she can illuminate as no one else can the private. This fact justifies her occasional omniscient intrusions into a world to which her scholars simply do not have access, and of these intrusions the final one, 'Postscript 1868', is also the *coup de grâce* that *Possession* delivers to the art of literary biography:

> There are things which happen and leave no discernible trace, are not spoken or written of, though it would be very wrong to say that subsequent events go on indifferently, all the same, as though such thing had never been.
>
> Two people met, on a hot May day, and never later mentioned their meeting. This is how it was. (*P.* 508)

5

Darwin and God

Angels and Insects consists of two novellas, 'Morpho Eugenia' and 'The Conjugial Angel'. The narrative connection around which the two stories (set respectively in the 1860s and the 1870s) pivot seems deliberately and challengingly attenuated, even wasp-waisted. At the end of 'Morpho Eugenia' the two remaining principal characters are last sighted midway across the Atlantic Ocean *en route* to the Amazon region on a ship under the captaincy of a newly introduced character, Captain Arturo Papagay. The second story leads us in, through the gifts of the medium Mrs Lilias Papagay, whom we must presume to be the widow of the captain (whose ship has gone missing, believed lost, in the Antarctic), to a reconstruction of the historically speaking scarcely documented response of Alfred Lord Tennyson's sister Mrs Emily Jesse, in her sixties, to the death of Arthur Henry Hallam, her former fiancé and immeasurably better known as the subject of Tennyson's *In Memoriam*, published in 1850, seventeen years after Hallam's death.

If the narrative connection seems tenuous, however, certain themes recur in the two stories, reinforcing each other's presence. Indeed, so persuasive are these themes, on further examination, that they force one to ask whether each story, taken in isolation, is quite the same as the effect of their juxtaposition under one title. The film *Angels and Insects*, which was released in 1995 and based on 'Morpho Eugenia', is certainly self-contained: yet the screenplay by Philip and Belinda Haas contains one significant addition to Byatt's plot and subjects it to one equally significant omission; these changes focus that story interestingly, as we shall see.

What are the themes connecting the two stories? We may think of them as matters that, while they have exercised a preoccupation on human civilization, probably for as long as it has been recognizable as such, came during the mid-nineteenth century to assume a particular urgency because of the erosion of the belief in a divine plan informing human creation by a more secularized view of the natural world associated (though by no means exclusively) with the name of Charles Darwin, whose *Origin of Species* first appeared in 1859. Yet nearly a decade earlier, Tennyson, examining, in *In Memoriam*, the idea of theodicy (the intractable problem of how a benevolent God can permit human suffering), had famously written, in remarkably Darwinian terms, of his (Tennyson's) agony at the intellectual discoveries that Hallam's death had seemed to imply:

> Are God and Nature then at strife,
>   That Nature lends such evil dreams?
>   So careful of the type she seems,
> So careless of the single life.
>
>   .   .   .   .
>
> 'So careful of the type'? But no.
>   From scarped cliff and quarried stone
>   She cries, 'A thousand types are gone:
> I care for nothing, all shall go.'

Some fifteen years later, the troubled enlightened liberal clergyman Sir Harald Alabaster, discoursing with his son-in-law the biologist William Adamson in 'Morpho Eugenia', reflects:

The world has changed so much, William, in my lifetime. I am old enough to have believed in our First Parents in Paradise, as a little boy, to have believed in Satan hidden in the snake, and in the Archangel with the flaming sword, closing the gates. I am old enough to have believed *without question* in the Divine Birth on a cold night with the sky full of singing angels and the shepherds staring up in wonder, and the strange kings advancing across the sand on camels with gifts. And now I am presented with a world in which we are what we are because of the mutations of soft jelly and calceous bone matter through unimaginable millennia – a world in which angels and devils do not battle in the heavens for virtue and vice, but in which we eat and are eaten and absorbed into each other[,] flesh and blood. ... I shall moulder like a mushroom when my time comes, which is not long. It is likely that the injunction to love each other is no more than the prudent instinct of sociability, of parental protectiveness, in a creature related to a great ape. (*AI* 59)

31

Alabaster is mourning, among other things, what he sees as the loss of certainties that include a sense of beauty, of a divinely ordained pattern in creation. We may think of Alabaster's mental torture as equivalent to that of the more agnostic characters in *Possession*, but it should not be forgotten that the aesthetic imaginations of late-twentieth-century neo-Darwinists such as Stephen Jay Gould have been fired by the discoveries to which their rejection, in turn, of Darwin's anthropocentrism have led them. Gould, spurning what he has called 'the pitfalls of biological determinism', proposes an evolutionary model that questions its necessary culmination in Man (and indeed in bilateral symmetry and pentadactylism), seeing in this so-called 'culmination' no innate 'improvement' over forms that have simply not survived. (In this way, as has been pointed out, Gould's possible worlds approach those of the Argentinian fabulist Jorge Luis Borges.) The neo-Darwinian Gould (though having far more material to go on than his nineteenth-century predecessors) nevertheless (and in contrast) shares with the Darwinian Adamson a sense of sheer wonder at the variety of observable life forms and behaviour. Yet Adamson is hamstrung by Darwinian anthropocentrism: able to provide secular explanations for patterns of communal life and reproductive behaviour, he is quite unable to cope with the implications of those patterns as he shockingly discovers them in the human community into which he has been taken up. It might be added that, in the 1960s in which *Babel Tower* is set, Byatt has the geneticist Luk Lysgaard-Peacock remark:

> There are puzzling things. If strict Darwinian theory was true, populations under the same selective pressures should become more and more genetically homogeneous – but this isn't so. They show a surprising genetic polymorphism. All sorts of forms persist when strict theory might suggest that they should have vanished. (*BT* 357)

Among the themes uniting the two stories in *Angels and Insects*, then, I propose we consider: what it is to give a name to a living creature; the biology of miscegenation and the question of what is natural and what unnatural, including the theme of the dead fiancé; and the unobserved character apparently hovering on the fringes of the story she or he is in, yet who comes to assume significance in a dramatic shift in *Gestalt*.

But first it is worth pausing to examine the tenuous narrative link as it is embodied in one piece of naming: Papagay. The word is common to a number of Indo-European languages (in many of which, from Spanish and Portuguese to Dutch, from Greek to Arabic and Persian, it still exists); its standard Middle English variant was 'popinjay', and in modern English the word has become 'parrot'. The parrot combines the variegated beauties of the butterflies and moths in 'Morpho Eugenia' and the bright, otherworldly coloured angels perceived by the medium Sophy Sheekhy in 'The Conjugial Angel'. It fits the racially miscegenated husband Arturo, a Hermes figure who supervises the transition from one world to another of William Adamson and Matty Crompton in 'Morpho Eugenia'. It also fits the socially unplaceable wife Lilias, capable, with the more active assistance of her young companion Sophy, of obliging the spiritual needs of a socially respectable upper middle-class clientele. That clientele includes the grieving mother Mrs Hearnshaw and Mrs Emily Jesse, formerly Tennyson, both of whom are presented as what are termed in 'The Conjugial Angel' figures who need 'the wherewithal to keep body and soul together, until the blessed moment when we step over the bourne to join those Others, Beyond' (*AI* 170). In their turn, these needs remind us of the concerns of *Possession*, of Ash's attempt to disrupt Mrs Lees's seance, which he refers to in a letter to Ruskin as his 'Gaza exploit' (*P*. 389). This can be interpreted as an act of patriarchal suppression, and a reader such as Maud Bailey might well be tempted to do so. Her intelligence would forbid her to see the effect as a crude manipulation of gender politics, however, for the reader never ascertains whether the seance is 'genuine'.

It is not surprising that there should have been such an interest in spiritualism at a time in which Darwinism was removing so much spiritual certainty: the inanimate but sensate communities of insects examined in 'Morpho Eugenia' have their counterpart in the angelic communities speculated on in 'The Conjugial Angel'. 'Morpho Eugenia' is itself centred on an act of naming: William Adamson has returned to England having lost most of his possessions in a shipwreck. In an early conversation with him, his sponsor Sir Harald speculates on the possibility that a future discovery might be made on his (Sir

33

Harald's) behalf, and Sir Harald thereby immortalized as 'some monstrous toad or savage seeming beetle ... – Bufo amazoniensis haraldii – Cheops nigrissimum alabastri – I like that, do not you?' (*AI* 18). William is able to oblige Sir Harald with some rare specimens of the Morpho butterfly that he has managed to salvage, and we are to assume that these have already been classified by Linnaeus: 'They are Morpho Eugenia, Sir Harald' (*AI* 19).

In 'The Conjugial Angel' the distraught Mrs Hearnshaw 'has just buried the fifth little Amy Hearnshaw in seven years – they had had brief lives ranging from three weeks to eleven months' (*AI* 167) ('So careful of the type she seems, So careless of the single life'). Specimens of Morpho Eugenia have been rescued and preserved in all their beauty to allow William to pay court to Sir Harald's daughter: five little Amy Hearnshaws, in contrast, are decomposing in the earth. In an interview after the publication of *The Virgin in the Garden*, Byatt confessed to Juliet Dusinberre:

> I have been haunted by the figure of Betty Maguire whose children were killed in an IRA attack, and eventually she killed herself, but not till she had tried to get over it in a very macabre way, by having another child and calling it by the same name as [one of] the dead one[s]. Van Gogh's mother did the same with him. He was born on the same day as a brother who had died a year earlier and whom she called Vincent Van Gogh, and she used to take him to look at the grave. (JD 194)

During a subsequent seance (which – like all Byatt's seance scenes – may or may not be 'genuine'), Mrs Hearnshaw, who is once more pregnant, is urged by the spirits of the dead Amys and through the mediumship of Mrs Papagay to call the new daughter 'Rosamund' (*AI* 198) (Mrs Papagay seems not to doubt that Mrs Hearnshaw is carrying a daughter). Will 'the type' thereby become 'the single life'? And what, in the context of Tennyson's lines, will be the future of that life?

As we know, it is no longer customary (as it was in previous ages with their high infant mortality) to give surviving later children the names of their earlier-deceased siblings. Still, naming as an act may be regarded as more or less proper. A controversial instance in 'The Conjugial Angel' revolves around

Emily Jesse's decision to name her eldest son Arthur Hallam in memory of her dead fiancé. Attitudes differ. For Mrs Papagay, influenced by the Swedenborgian beliefs of the sexually predatory Mr Hawke, Emily's act is 'a gage of perpetuity, a Life-in-Death for the dead lover, an assertion of the wondrous community of the Spirit World, for believers' (*AI* 175). (Elizabeth Barrett – this is prior to her marriage with Robert Browning – is, in contrast, shocked at what she sees as the impropriety of the naming, as well as of Emily Jesse continuing to receive a £300 annuity from Hallam's father even after her marriage.) Mrs Papagay's favourite Tennyson poem is 'Enoch Arden', which in her mind has become identified with a narrative in which a sailor, missing presumed dead, returns to find his wife married to 'his hated cousin and mother of many little ones with his features but not his' (*AI* 176). At the end of 'The Conjugial Angel' Captain Arturo Papagay does indeed return, happily. Yet, in contrast, the non-seance-like imagined ending of Mrs Papagay's 'aborted novel' (*AI* 176) will strike the reader much more forcefully as a horrible disfiguring of the experience that overcomes William Alabaster at the end of 'Morpho Eugenia'. William's discovery of his wife Eugenia's incestuous affair with her brother Edgar since long before his marriage to Eugenia forces William to contemplate that none of their children may be his. Edgar's animal convictions about not sullying the bloodlines, his obsessions with breeding horses and hounds, have spilt disturbingly over into his own sexual prac-tice. As William says to Matty Crompton: 'I have never felt – not in my heart of hearts – any warmth to all those – white children – ' (*AI* 155). The miscegenation proper to the human (and 'higher' animal) species does not extend to the insect kingdom – nor does it seem to play a role in the love-making of angels. It is Emanuel Swedenborg who has coined the phrase 'conjugial love' to show that this love-making 'correspond[s] to the Union between Christ and His Church' (*AI* 175).

In a historical period where remarriage by a man to his deceased wife's sister was legally an act of incest, it is not surprising to find that the behaviour expected of women engaged to male partners who have died during the engage-ment period and before marriage comes under intense scrutiny. The fact that Eugenia's fiancé has died is at first presented, then held at the edges of our attention, before finally being explained and made sense of, throughout the course of 'Morpho Eugenia':

> 'Captain Hunt . . . saw – he saw – oh, not so much as *you* have seen – but enough to guess. And it preyed on his mind. . . . And he wrote a terrible letter – to – to both of us – and said – oh – ' she began to weep rapidly suddenly, 'he could not live with the knowledge even if *we* could. . . . And then he shot himself. In his desk there was a note, to me, saying I would know why he had died, and that he hoped I would be able to be happy.' (*AI* 150–1)

Reading 'The Conjugial Angel' between the same set of covers as we read 'Morpho Eugenia', it is difficult for us to avoid the slight *frisson* of distaste as Emily Jesse reconstructs for us the Hallam she has known – as opposed to the one *In Memoriam* has immortalized. We are also made aware of the possibility that another nineteenth-century taboo – an improper affection between two men – has been breached, which makes us ask whether Emily has not figuratively speaking committed a form of unconsummated incest by virtue of her engagement to Arthur Hallam. More important still for present purposes is the assertion that Emily 'could never be wholly easy about the way in which Alfred's mourning had overtaken her own. Had not only overtaken it, she told herself in moments of bleak truthfulness, had undone and denied it' (*AI* 229).

Emily's attempts to reclaim this experience recall Byatt's own remarks, in the interview with Juliet Dusinberre, about not wishing to be appropriated into any kind of political agenda, feminist or otherwise: to submit would be 'a denial of real fertility and real freedom' (JD 186). Those attempts also parallel, in 'The Conjugial Angel', Mrs Papagay's belief throughout the story that she is widowed and that her partner is irreplaceable. A comparable strength is shown by Matty Crompton, who hovers on the edges of William Adamson's apprehension of the events that comprise 'Morpho Eugenia'. The idea is familiar enough: it is a recapitulation of the plot of *David Copperfield*. The sidelined woman, and the strength she is able to provide the story's hero, a strength absent from the story's apparent heroine, is what the story turns out to have been about. The Haas screenplay of *Angels and Insects* adds a persuasive focusing element: in Byatt's 'Morpho Eugenia', Sir Harald has married twice, and his first wife is the mother of Edgar, Eugenia, Rowena, and Enid; after her death (before the story has begun) Sir Harald remarries, begetting further offspring by the second Lady Alabaster. In the film, Lady Alabaster is a composite figure, gross, sedentary, Queen Bee-like. Introducing her death towards the end of the film as part of the plot allows Haas to underline the parallel whereby the queen's death leads to the dissolution of the colony.

The Haas screenplay omits Mattie Crompton's insect-inspired fairy-tale 'Things Are Not What They Seem', presumably also in the interests of focus. In the novella 'Morpho Eugenia' Matty's story prepares both William, and us as readers, for her resourcefulness at the end. She has been the kind of unobserved woman to which a later chapter of this essay is devoted: unlike the examples discussed there, however, she is neither menopausal nor even middle-aged. Her challenge to William (not wholly unlike that posed by Christabel LaMotte to Randolph Henry Ash) is an imposing gamble informed by sexual good manners yet constantly invigorated with a sharpness that acts as a metaphor for what William has more than once noticed as her spicy tang, a palpable olfactory sexuality utterly lacking in Eugenia. As he listens to Matty's version of the story in her attic room, in her own space where she is no longer 'Matty' or 'Miss Crompton' but Matilda, William is told:

> 'There are people in houses, between the visible inhabitants and the invisible, largely invisible to *both*, who can know a very great deal, or nothing, as they choose. I choose to know about some things, and not to know about others. I have become interested in knowing things that concern you.' . . .
>
> She rose, and began to pace, like a prisoner in a cell, in a little room. He was quiet, watching her. She said, 'You do not know that I am a woman. Why should that not continue as it is? You have *never seen me.*'
>
> Her voice had a new harshness, a new note. She said, 'You have no idea who I am. You have no idea even how old I am. Have you? You think I may be of an age between thirty and fifty, confess it.'
>
> 'And if you know so precisely what I think, it is because you must have meant me to think it.'
>
> What she had said was nevertheless true. He had no idea, and that was what he had thought. She paced on. William said, 'Tell me then, since you invite the question, how old are you?'

'I am twenty-seven,' said Matty Crompton. 'I have only one life, and twenty-seven years of it are past, and I intend to begin living.' (*AI* 155–7)

The fairy tale omitted, for whatever reason, in the Haas screenplay of *Angels and Insects* is an essential part of the make-up of *Possession*, as well as returning in, and characterizing, *The Djinn in the Nightingale's Eye*. It is to this aspect of Byatt's work, and to its context in contemporary British writing, that we now turn.

6

Wonder-Tales

Randolph Henry Ash's incomplete poem 'Mummy Possest', read by the twentieth-century feminists in *Possession* as an outspokenly misogynistic attack on the seance he has disrupted at Mrs Lees's, offers a simile that is revealing for what it suggests about A. S. Byatt's attitude to the fairy tale:

> Our small deceptions are a form of Art
> Which has its simple and its high degree
> As women know, who lavish on wax dolls
> The skills and the desires that large-souled men
> Save up for marble Cherubs, or who sew
> On lowly cushions thickets of bright flowers
> Which done in oils were marvelled at on walls
> Of ducal halls or city galleries.
> You call these spirit *mises en scène* a lie.
> I call it artfulness, or simply Art,
> A Tale, a Story, that may hide a Truth
> As wonder-tales do, even in the Best Book.

(*P.* 408–9)

Recently Marina Warner, in an edited collection entitled *Wonder Tales* (1994), to which Byatt herself contributed a translation of Marie-Catherine d'Aulnoy's *Le Serpentin vert* (1698), has argued that the appellation 'wonder tales' conduces more to the feel of the marvellous, and is indeed in every way less constricting, in conveying the sense of what are more usually referred to in English as 'fairy tales' or 'fairy stories'. Interestingly, Christabel LaMotte uses 'Wonder Tale' in a letter to Ash (*P.* 160). Warner reminds us that 'wonder tales' (*Wundermärchen*) draws on the German (and by extension Russian) sense of the term's own identity, whereas it is the French *conte des fées* that has supplied the English language with its more customary, restraining, term.

Certainly 'wonder tales' seems appropriate to those stories of Byatt's that are embedded in larger narratives. Warner's little etymological explanation reminds us of the pan-European nature of the wonder tale, and in her work in and since *Possession* Byatt draws on several aspects of European tradition and indeed beyond. *Possession* itself contains, in the work of Christabel LaMotte, tales that reflect her own French and particularly Breton ancestry – as she tells her cousin Sabine de Kercoz:

> Since I came here, I have not attempted to write anything, because I do not know what language to think in. I am like the Fairy Mélusine, the Sirens and the Mermaids, half-French, half-English and behind these languages the Breton and the Celt. (*P.* 348)

Christabel LaMotte also tells wonder tales that show the Germanic influence of Tieck and the brothers Grimm. Ash's work extends the terms of reference to Norse tradition, although it would be more accurate to consider this material mythological rather than wondrous. Surely this pan-Europeanism was one of the elements contributing to *Possession*'s remarkable international success. Two of Christabel's wonder tales, 'The Glass Coffin' and 'Gode's Story', are reprinted in *The Djinn in the Nightingale's Eye*, the title of this collection reminding us that more than half of it is taken up with Byatt's only excursion to date into Oriental folklore. Interestingly the collection is subtitled 'Five Fairy Stories'.

The stories in *The Djinn and the Nightingale's Eye* are all self-contained. Accomplished as they are, it will be my assumption in this chapter that Byatt's fairy stories really only become true wonder tales when, in Ash's words, they 'hide a Truth... even in the Best Book'. I take these words to justify my concentration not on the self-containedness or integrity of given stories, but on the ways in which they are incorporated into larger narratives, and on what happens when one tries to unpack them from those narratives. In other words, 'The Glass Coffin' and 'Gode's Story', even though reprinted word for word in *The Djinn in the Nightingale's Eye*, are quite different in nature from their incorporated or embedded 'originals' in *Possession*. Nor do I mean to suggest that those originals are straightforwardly didactic in nature, that they have only what Matty Crompton calls 'too much *message*' (*AI* 141). Instead I shall return to the conversation Matty holds with William Adamson following his (and of course our) reading of 'Things Are Not What They Seem', focusing on a more elusive and mysterious aspect of Byatt's craft, the quality Ash terms 'artfulness', and on the sense of the marvellous that his simile seems to imply.

Matty Crompton's 'Things Are Not What They Seem' enhances and redefines her place in *Angels and Insects*. It also attempts – along with the various stories in *Possession* (Christabel's wonder tales, such as 'The Glass Coffin', 'The Threshold', and, of course, 'The Fairy Melusina' itself, as well as the remarkable 'Gode's Story') – to unsettle its readers by thwarting expectations both as to the twists and turns generic fairy tales are supposed to take as well as to any presuppositions such readers may have entertained about the teller. Marina Warner's recent writing has focused on the marginalized position of the almost invariably female teller. Both Byatt and Warner have acknowledged their indebtedness to the work of the American folklore scholar Jack Zipes, but both argue more immediately that they were strongly influenced by Angela Carter's timely and original reintroduction of the marvellous, in its fairy-tale or wonder-tale manifestations, into contemporary British fiction during the 1970s. Carter's pioneering collection *The Bloody Chamber* (1979) stylishly and mischievously feminized familiar stories such as 'Bluebeard's Castle', 'Little Red Riding Hood', and 'Puss-in-Boots'.

Matty Crompton's wonder tale lives up to its title in a number of ways. The young hero Seth, arriving in and then attempting to escape from the Circe-like earthly paradise of Dame Cottitoe Pan Demos, must learn that this fairy is not what she seems. The various Helpers who enable his escape repeatedly impress on Seth the lesson carried in the title. Matty's tale contains many of the morphological trappings of the wonder tale (the supernatural, creatures that speak, a dream-like setting, an enigmatic riddle to be solved), but the coursings of Seth's adventures are complex and unpredictable.

The real originality of 'Things Are Not What They Seem' lies in its examination of naming. At one stage Mistress Mouffet explains to Seth: 'Names, you know, are a way of weaving the world together, by relating the creatures to other creatures and a kind of *metamorphosis*, you might say, out of a *metaphor* which is a figure of speech for carrying one idea into another' (*AI* 132). We may admire the elegance with which the word 'metaphor' is actually contained in the word 'metamorphosis' as much as we may admire the profundity of the thought. Seth is transformed to the size of an insect: a story imaginatively written in the early 1860s appropriately contains more than faint echoes of Lewis Carroll and Charles Kingsley. Mistress Mouffett makes clear that Seth has been 'misreading' the insects he sees. In this way he is frightened by the Large Elephant Hawk Moth that is to transport him to the great Fairy, the asker of riddles, as soon as the Moth spreads its wings to reveal the death's head that is its protection. Asking Miss Mouffet, 'What is *this* Moth's true name?', he is told: 'It is the Death's-head Hawk, Sphinx Acherontia Atropos' (*AI* 136). All these creatures have acquired names during the course of human history, names that describe what they signify to a given culture; more recently and systematically, they have also been subjected to Linnaean classification. But the Linnaean system, though admittedly one of unprecedented sophistication, is actually no different from the old haphazard namings in the sense that it, too, must rely on metaphor: there is never a 'real' unmediated abstract terminology available, in a world of signs, that does not itself draw on signification.

Trying to account for what she sees as the uncharacteristic fluency of her story, Matty tells William how struck she had been by the name Large Elephant Hawk Moth:

'And I thought that the thing was a kind of *walking figure of speech* – and began to look up the etymologies – and found it was all running away from me. It was as though I was dragged along willy-nilly – by the *language*, you know – through Sphinx and Morpheus and Thomas Mouffet – I suppose my *Hermes* was Linnaeus – who does not appear.'

'It is all extremely ingenious, certainly.'

'I am afraid,' said Miss Crompton carefully, 'that it is too didactic. That there is too much *message*. Did you find that there was too much message?'

'I don't think that is true, no. The impression I got from it was one of thickening *mystery*, like the riddle of the Sphinx herself, a most portentous person. I think childish readers will find both instruction and delight in it.' (*AI* 141)

The combination of instruction and delight is an aim with a noble and classical history, but with this last observation William has moved smartly onto safer ground. He has extricated himself from the much more suggestive but disturbing possibility this exegetic conversation is debating, which is that the true wonder tale must somehow manage to hover suspensefully between 'message' and 'thickening mystery'. Let us devote the remainder of this chapter to a brief examination of two of the wonder tales in *Possession* itself in order to test this possibility.

My assertion that 'The Glass Coffin' and 'Gode's Story' are absolutely transformed by their existence within the narrative matrix of *Possession*, even though the wording of the tales may be identical outside that context in *The Djinn in the Nightingale's Eye*, aims to support the view that in Byatt's work the wonder tale negotiates a path of its own between 'message' and 'thickening mystery'. The case of 'The Glass Coffin' is more straightforward than is that of 'Gode's Story', as we shall see, so we will take 'The Glass Coffin' first.

The frame story of 'The Glass Coffin' involves a resourceful tailor who is offered a choice of three gifts by a 'little grey man' across whose forest dwelling he comes while looking for work. It is a conventional tale with a self-confessedly unconventional twist: that is, that the gift the tailor chooses, the glass key, while admittedly the third he is offered, is one he admits he has never encountered in the genre within which he finds himself. The frame encloses a variation on the Sleeping Beauty, whom the tailor awakes from her glass coffin with the use of the glass key. The Sleeping Beauty narrative may be making some comment – and the livelier exegetes within *Possession* would certainly find comment irresistible – on the status of Christabel, the teller of the tale. The enchantment under which the young woman has been placed (she automatically assumes the tailor to be her Prince, although her own precise status is withheld from the reader) has arisen out of the interruption of her idyllic life with her brother by a 'black artist', who visits the castle in which they live and wishes to come between the lady and her brother. The black artist achieves his aim by turning the brother into the dog, Otto, who now lives in the little grey man's household, and by incarcerating the Princess in her glass coffin, from which the tailor rescues her with his glass key.

Exegesis of the tale might well take some such form as this: Christabel (the lady) is trying to expiate her guilt at the fate of Blanche Glover (the muted Otto), who has committed suicide under the conviction that she has become superfluous now that Ash (the black artist) has disrupted the idyllic life the two women have led at Richmond. So interpreted, the story would become a kind of wish-fulfilment fantasy in which Blanche/Otto is restored to life and language, whereas Ash is haplessly written out of the affair. In the tale, the black artist fails to guard himself when confronted by the tailor, who deftly kills him using a shard of the glass coffin. The black artist 'shrivelled and withered under their eyes, and became a small handful of grey dust and glass powder' (P. 67). We will learn towards the end of *Possession* that during the period immediately after the birth of Maia, who has been surrendered to her aunt Sophie Bailey, Christabel has felt intense and impotent anger at Ash and deep remorse at the fate of Blanche. In this sense, at least, 'The Glass Coffin' attains a resonance within *Possession* that it simply cannot have when excised from it.

An oddity in the story, both in its 'self-contained' and in its contextualized version, is provided by the fate (and thus by implication the interpretative status) of the little grey man, who vanishes from the narrative after the denouement. This kind of veiled puzzlement seems inherent in Christabel's story-telling strategy, which I have already claimed disrupts conventional generic expectations, and in so doing probes the ways in which 'message' can metamorphose into 'thickening mystery'. Christabel is in the habit of offering her readers asides, of which perhaps the most striking in 'The Glass Coffin' occurs when the tailor declines the lady's offer of marriage (which is freely made by her, not extorted from her, as in the case of the black artist): 'why you should have me, simply because I opened the glass case, is less clear to me altogether' – these words from the tailor are not what the genre leads its readers to expect. Christabel picks up this uncomfortable ambivalence of power and social and sexual position, and gives it a tweak of her own: 'And you may ask yourselves, my dear and most innocent readers, whether he spoke there with more gentleness or cunning, since the lady set such store on giving herself of her own free will ...' (P. 66). In isolation this would be 'the narrator's voice'. Knowing it, as we do, to be Christabel's voice, we are offered further evidence that we are in the company of a writer who likes to disconcert, to let things jar, a writer who is anything but bland, a writer who sends her messages clothed in thickening mystery. Another example, if one were needed, is provided in 'The Threshold', which contains an ostensibly conventional choice between gold, silver, and lead. Christabel wistfully imagines 'a moment's true sorrow for ... the sunlit flowery earth which is my own secret preference' before submitting to the conventional expectations of these wonder tales, although not without a struggle: 'And one day we will write it otherwise ... But you must know now, that it turned out as it must turn out, must you not? Such is the power of necessity in tales' (P. 155).

The mysterious story told by Gode is told by a character whom Marina Warner would immediately recognize as marginal: Gode is a servant with preternatural wisdom and foresight; she is described as a 'witch' (P. 346) and intuits Christabel's pregnancy before anyone else does in the Breton household where Christabel has sought sanctuary; she is in touch with the spirit world – at Toussaint, according to Sabine de Kercoz, which initiates the Breton story-telling period that continues until Christmas:

> Gode always joins us and tells us of the year's trafficking between this world and *that*, the other side of the threshold, which at Toussaint may be crossed in both directions, by live men walking into that world, and by spies, or outposts, or messengers sent from There to our brief daylight. (P. 353)

Sabine recognizes that Gode's culture is oral not written, and that Gode's story will lose in the writing-down what animates it in the telling. Sabine is also aware that Toussaint is the time for stories that should not have '[t]oo much meaning' (P. 355). She recalls how a visitor once told a 'dead tale, a neat little political allegory ... and it was as though a net had drawn up a shoal of dull dead fish with loose scales, no one knew where to look, or how to smile' (P. 353).

45

There is thus a social protocol in the Toussaint tale-telling that suggests that the unlearned, orally skilled storytellers weave the most suggestively opaque stories. Yet Sabine's father, Raoul, despite being scholarly and aristocratic, knows that the multiply-named place that is the setting for a given tale

> 'shifts its borders and the directions of its dark rides and wooded alleys – it cannot be pinned down or fixed, any more than can its invisible inhabitants and magical properties, but it is always there, and all these names indicate only one time or aspect of it . . .' (P. 353)

In this way Raoul's customary telling of the tale of Merlin and Vivien is 'always the same tale, never twice the same telling' (P. 353). This multivalent inaccessible obscurity attracts Sabine: 'I do not believe all these *explanations*. They diminish. The idea of woman is less than brilliant Vivien, and the idea of Merlin will not allegorise into male wisdom. He is Merlin' (P. 355).

Here, then, we have a situation that is more complex than the case of 'The Glass Coffin'. Reprinted in *The Djinn in the Nightingale's Eye*, 'Gode's Story' (like 'The Glass Coffin') is absolutely recalcitrant to the kind of exegesis that ingenious readers of – and in – *Possession* will try to bring to it. On the basis of Sabine's testimony, the Breton culture in which Gode tells her story appears to be one that also rejects 'too much meaning', yet Sabine does not know what she will come to know (however dimly and partially), what Gode appears intuitively to know, what the twentieth-century scholars will know less enigmatically still, and what readers of *Possession* are offered as virtual omniscience by a tricksy narrator. In short, 'Gode's Story', embedded in *Possession* in the way it is, rejects interpretation in the terms of its own culture, but seems to speak to Christabel in a 'meaningful' way, and *thus* forces the exercise of exegetical effort from the omniscient reader.

Such a reader would see Gode's story as her divination that Christabel is carrying a child. The miller's daughter wishes to put a price on the ribbon she is given by the young sailor; he is insulted and sets as that price 'Sleepless nights till I come again' (P. 358). The sailor stays away and the miller's daughter wastes away; in the meantime, in a curious episode that suggests and repels 'meaning', the miller, hearing a noise one night in his barn, wakes his daughter to discover 'blood on the straw'. Finally rejected by the miller's daughter, the sailor becomes involved with Jeanne, the smith's daughter, while the miller's daughter appears to hear 'little bare feet, dancing' (P. 359). On the night of the sailor's marriage to Jeanne, the miller's daughter is seen in her shift running after something and calling upon it to wait for her – is it 'a tiny naked child dancing and prancing in front of her' or 'nothing but a bit of blown dust whirling in the road'? (P. 360). All we are told for certain is that the apparition leads the miller's daughter over the edge of a cliff to her death on the rocks below. The sailor, hearing the pattering feet at Toussaint, becomes obsessed by the phantom child and journeys with it to the Baie des Trépassés, one of the few remaining places 'where two worlds cross' (P. 355). Distressed by the crowding-in upon him of the Dead, the sailor feels completely unable to board the boat that takes the child into the other world. The sailor in turn waits and wastes, and when he has apparently waited longer than the miller's daughter or the little child had been prepared to do, he dies.

It seems that Christabel is as able (or desperate enough) to unpack meaning from Gode's story as Sabine is reluctant to, although Sabine cannot possibly know this, and indeed misreads the way in which Christabel is clearly moved by the story as 'evidence' that Christabel and Raoul are becoming emotionally attached to each other and that Christabel is about to become that stock wonder-tale figure: the stepmother.

Yet in its totality (and only in its totality) *Possession* permits the exegetical possibility that the sailor stands for Ash, as the miller's daughter does for Christabel, and that the insult to the sailor's gift and the repeated injunctions to wait, along with the discovery of blood in the barn, point to the complicit concealment of the pregnancy that has followed Christabel's defloration. The introduction of the phantom child enhances Gode's prescience by leading forward to the mystery of what has happened during Christabel's subsequent confinement and to Ash's disruption of Mrs Lees's seance. The Baie des Trépassés, the place where worlds cross, takes on an extra hermeneutical significance whereby those two worlds can be identified as the world of past and present, of real historical characters and their would-be biographers, of fiction and reality.

47

7

**'Real Accident':
Plotting and Pattern**

In a 'Postface' written in February 1991 commending the elegance of Jean-Louis Chevalier's translation of two of the stories from *Sugar and Other Stories*, 'The July Ghost' and 'Precipice-Encurled', A. S. Byatt argues that those stories have more in common than ostensibly meets the eye. She continues:

> J'ai commencé à réfléchir à la manière de dépeindre un accident *réel* selon l'ordre de l'art en 1961, année de la naissance de mon fils. J'avais lu dans la presse un article sur une femme dont les deux enfants étaient morts noyés en même temps, et je m'étais fait, dans une note, l'observation personnelle qu'il serait presque impossible à une œuvre de fiction de ne pas laisser pressentir, présager ou entrevoir à l'avance une raison morale à un tel événement, qui changeait la nature de tout au monde pour une femme comme celle-ci, pour toujours, et du jour au lendemain. Je commençai à concevoir un roman, *Nature morte*, où surviendrait un accident *réel*, de cette sorte. Mon fils fut tué par une voiture en 1972, et *Nature morte* parut finalement en 1985. *Le Fantôme de juillet* a été écrit huit ans après la mort de mon fils, au moment où il sembla recommencer à être possible d'imaginer un garçon de cet âge. (*Fdj* 85–6)

The reference to the article in the press actually found its way via Byatt's notebooks into the composition of *Still Life*. Stephanie Potter, mother of a baby son, reads the newspapers (like many young parents):

> with a sense of urgency because she now lived in the world they described, a world of human events, births, accidents, marriages, deaths. She ... had wept for the woman whose two children had been found drowned in a flooded quarry, who had been transformed between morning and evening, and in five lines of print, from a

woman, any woman, with two children, to a woman whose past pointed towards this terrible present, whose future was the afterlife of this absolute accidental blow. (*SL* 280)

One senses, in the precise timing recollected in the genesis of Byatt's thoughts about 'real accident' and its representation in art, that after it tragically overtook her in reality with the death of her 11-year-old son Charles in 1972, Byatt began to wonder whether she had in some way 'called it down'. In the 'Postface', written nearly twenty years after the event itself, she is steadfastly facing this possibility even as she recalls her earlier grappling with the difficulty of truthfully depicting a *real* accident in fiction.

Byatt had been impressed by one of the best English novels of the later 1950s. Angus Wilson's *The Middle Age of Mrs Eliot* (1958) attracted her because of its extraordinarily engaging portrait of a middle-aged widow, an achievement that was warmly acknowledged in reviews of Wilson's novel. The charismatic and resourceful Mrs Eliot is widowed after her husband is shot dead in an airport restaurant as they are beginning a long holiday to the Far East.

This event comes as a shock to the reader, it is true, but it could be argued that, in terms of the novel's form, the concept of 'real accident' is impaired. That is to say, Mr Eliot's death is not really an accident at all, in formal terms, because it has been planned by the novelist *in order to set up the plot*. The purpose of that plot is that Mrs Eliot's independence should be seen to ripen. In terms of the novel's form, the accident could thus be regarded as a stratagem designed to enable Wilson's plot to come to fruition.

It is as well to establish what we mean by 'plot' before proceeding further. In his *Aspects of the Novel* (1927) E. M. Forster, who had given the matter much thought, wrote that the difference between *story* and *plot* was that in addition to *story*'s narrative telling us a sequence of events ('The king died and then the queen died' is Forster's example), *plot* adds the element of *causality* ('[T]he king died and then the queen died of grief'). Let us contrast Wilson's portrayal of an accident with the opening sentence of the fifth chapter of Forster's *The Longest Journey* (1907): 'Gerald died that afternoon.' The shock these words deliver to the reader really is very great indeed. The words are absolutely unexpected, and the shock is that much greater than that brought about by the death of Wilson's Mr Eliot. But why is this actually so? One answer may be that Wilson has inscribed, or has had his plot lead up to, the death of Mr Eliot primarily in order to open up sufficient imaginative space for the enterprising construction of Mrs Wilson. Only secondarily, as it were, is the reader hit in the face by events. Mrs Wilson as widow is enabled to assume an identity that she could not have had as Mrs Wilson as partner. Hitting the reader in the face with his announcement of Gerald's death in a game of football is, in contrast, the *primary* effect achieved by Forster.

While the remainder of *The Longest Journey* (subtly and sometimes puzzlingly) follows its central character Rickie into his relationship with Agnes Pembroke, the girl originally destined to marry Gerald Dawes, the plot is of a complexity that could not really be foreseen. Marriage between Rickie and Agnes is not explicitly what Gerald has died *for*, in terms of the novel's plot. In contrast, Mrs Eliot (as her very name reveals) is defined by the accident in her life: that accident is central to the life as plotted by Wilson. The accidental death of Gerald leads Rickie into marriage with Agnes in such a way as to permit Forster's working out of a plot apprehensible as one of a number of imaginable possibilities. In the event Rickie, a writer sharing many of the qualities we admire in Forster, allows himself to be steered off course by Agnes. He is not strong enough to maintain his own fragile integrity and ends up conforming to the stiflingly complacent social conventions that Forster satirizes in so much of his work.

What do these two examples imply about their authors' attitudes to their principal characters? Although Wilson's fictional treatment of accident attracted Byatt because of the way it enables a middle-aged widow to construct herself in a society that would otherwise have had little use for her, Forster's technique – it seems fair to suggest – possesses a more numinous, mysterious quality that forbids his more interesting characters to reveal themselves fully: they remain opaque to the reader. Nevertheless, neither example – courageous though each in its way was – can have seemed quite satisfactory to Byatt, because each (if one may put it this way) requires the disposal of one character rather early on in the story in order to advance the plot. Yet it cannot surely be the case that accidents in fiction *must* preclude their plots' giving a fully independent respectful existence of the distinctive otherness of the character who had been removed.

If this was, as her 'Postface' to the Chevalier translations suggest, the formal question puzzling Byatt as early as 1961, she was finally able to confront it head-on in *Still Life*, the sequel to *The Virgin in the Garden*, completed (according to her account) over two decades after she had first conceived it. For the appalling truth facing the reader of *Still Life* is that Stephanie Orton *née* Potter's death is not *necessary* to the plot, as those of Mr Eliot and Gerald are (in different ways) to theirs. No consolation is to be derived from arguing that the death of Stephanie enables those who are left to make any sense out of it. Nor is any kind of sentimentality allowed to intrude. Even though, as we shall see, patterns can be discerned, their purpose is not to console so much as to reflect desolately on an inscrutable universe.

Let us consider this point briefly. A marvellous passage from Bede accompanies the dedication of *Still Life*:

> 'Such,' he said, 'O King, seems to me the present life of men on earth, in comparison with that time which to us is uncertain, as if when on a winter's night you sit feasting with your ealdormen and thegns – a single sparrow should fly swiftly into the hall, and coming in at one door, fly out through another. Soon, from winter going back into winter, it is lost to your eyes.'

In the mess that follows the accident, we see Byatt's characters thinking their way through (not necessarily, or not yet, 'out of') what has hit them.

Indeed, *Still Life* actually *mocks*, retrospectively, any attempt to make sense of Stephanie's death. The major character whose role is most opaque in the entire novel is Stephanie's younger brother Marcus, who has been involved with the potentially deranged schoolmaster Lucas Simmonds in *The Virgin and the Garden* by virtue of Marcus's apparently preternatural gifts of sensory perception. Through much of *Still Life* Marcus remains in a clinically disturbed state, living away from his parents with

Stephanie and her curate husband Daniel. Cloistered for much of the time in his room, he emerges only to be baited by Daniel's arthritic and tetchy mother on account of his faddiness about appetite and his general physical incompetence, on one hideously farcical occasion specifically because he is unable to change the baby Will. Meanwhile Daniel's parish has acquired a new vicar, Gideon Farrar, who with his wife Clemency is coarse-grainedly committed to a 1950s version of muscular Christian socialism, to be transformed, in *Babel Tower* in the 1960s, into a charismatic evangelism. At Gideon's behest, Marcus becomes involved with a community known as the Young People in the parish. His closest approach to happiness in the entire novel occurs during this time, when, while sketching in an elm grove, he experiences an *Aha-Erlebnis*, defined after it has occurred as something as a result of which 'a structure felt to be defective or inchoate suddenly appears formed and harmonious' (*SL* 293). How does this come about?

Marcus seems about to enter the environs of normal human experience once more, as he discovers the beauty of the form of an elm tree ('He registered happiness . . . He considered the tree. . . . The leaves were alive . . . The veining pleased him' (*SL* 290)). An obscure but important passage follows:

> When he had become ill, he had had a time of terror in a field of pouring light, had felt himself to be some kind of funnel through which the light must flow, his eye a burning glass. He had devised a kind of geometric scheme to make the thing safe to think about, two intersecting cones, at the centre of which his eye, his mind almost accidentally were. He held his hand against the tree-skin, working out that he was back in the same place, seen differently. Only he was not afraid. He was not afraid, moreover, for two clear reasons. One was that the tree, the tree itself, was the intersection, the meeting cones, between light and earth. (The word 'earthed' came into his mind with a kind of silly coherence.) The other was that he was now, however imperfectly, equipped to *think* about this, to map its order. (*SL* 291)

The full meaningless of that 'silly coherence' will become evident to the reader, if not to Marcus. It sits in Byatt's text as accident does in her plot.

In the plot as in life we as readers are wrong-footed. Marcus appears to be approaching something akin to 'normality' with the Young People. There is busyness in Stephanie's life that has to do with the preparation of a nativity play. People come in and out of the house, and 'It was at this point that the white cat brought in the sparrow' (*SL* 399). The bird is revived, but concerted attempts to get it out of the house prove unavailing. Eventually, the parish helpers leave, Daniel is still occupied on pastoral business, Stephanie cooks for and bathes her children, reads to Will, and makes coffee for Marcus when he comes in much later. (Daniel is still not home.) Stephanie and Marcus make another attempt to get the sparrow out of the house, but it panics and ends up under the refrigerator. Pulling the refrigerator away from the wall, Stephanie just about manages to reach the sparrow.

> And then the refrigerator struck. She thought, as the pain ran through her, as her arm, fused to the metal, burned and banged, as her head filled, 'This is it' and then, with a flashing vision of heads on pillows, 'Oh, what will happen to the children?' And then the word, altruism, and surprise at it. And then dark pain, and more pain. (*SL* 403)

Daniel (Marcus later reflects) would not have been frozen into inaction as Marcus himself is, but Daniel is not there to intervene. Eventually, as in the nature of things, help is sought and found, and '[t]he little house filled with people. Ambulance men ... attempted artificial respiration. ... It was no good, the ambulance men said.' And then Daniel enters, unknowing, 'frowning with surprise, suspicion, irritation at seeing Gideon and Marcus, over whose heads a sudden sparrow plunged into the night' (*SL* 404). We are back to the passage from Bede, and further still, to the beginning of *The Virgin in the Garden*. Our first glimpse of Stephanie, the Cambridge graduate, has been of her in her parents' house attempting to rescue the remaining half of a litter of kittens whose mother has been panicked into death at the Vicarage; Daniel, the young curate, had then come to enquire after them and to express thanks, and had been fiercely rebuffed by the atheistic Bill Potter.

Now, at the end of *Still Life* (*Nature morte*), Daniel wakes up the next morning. 'He remembered. This was the first time he had had to remember and therefore the brightest and rawest, like the indifferent sunlight' (*SL* 405). In his dogged practical way he has known, the previous evening, that

> [h]e must *make this be true* for himself, relentless, no lies, no consolations of fantasy. Bill answered the telephone.
> 'Yes?'
> 'It's Daniel.' He could not find even a mitigating preparatory sentence, could not bear to speak a few half-true words which might allow Bill to contemplate the possibility of death before its fact. 'I have rung to tell you that Stephanie has been accidentally killed. In the kitchen. The refrigerator was not earthed.' (*SL* 406)

We remember the 'silly coherence' with which, in the elm grove, the word 'earthed' had come to Marcus's mind, and we realize that we are in the presence of one of those rarest of writers in whose fictional universe connections can be created and discerned as in some glorious medieval *liber creaturarum*, but for whom instead pattern most emphatically does not 'mean', or even necessarily begin to offer, consolation. Later, in *Babel Tower*, we will see how Stephanie's death has traumatized, in very different ways, specifically Daniel (who abandons his children and is quite simply unable to communicate with Marcus) and Frederica (who embarks on a disastrously incompatible marriage with Nigel Reiver because he was the only person able to comfort her).

Byatt thus disagrees with Virginia Woolf's view of the world impinging itself upon us as a series of random impressions: she has recently admitted that she has come to see life as a vulnerable twisted knot that eventually gets cut off. (Stephanie's thoughts while dying are an attempt to represent this.) The extraordinary nature of the artistic achievement this insight embodies cannot be overstressed. It is made possible only by Byatt's moral honesty, which is of the highest order, coupled with her conviction that her characters must be depicted as having thoughts, that those thoughts are frequently important, exciting, and painful, and that neither the act nor the depiction of thinking must be confused with specious attempts to make sense of the world.

8

'Visible but Unseen': Menopause and Marginalization

Few contemporary writers have examined both patriarchal and social attitudes to marginalized women more imaginatively than A. S. Byatt. *Still Life*, for instance, scrutinizes with real particularity the lives of Winifred Potter and of the mother of Daniel Orton. Of the latter, her son's brother-in-law Marcus can remark to himself: 'She is *no* use. . . . She does not want to be of use. She eats' (*SL* 162).

Two kinds of manifestation of this aspect of Byatt's work stand out. There is, firstly, a – chiefly patriarchal – demonization that guides the fates of several of the female characters in *Possession*. Secondly, there are forms of marginalization for which Byatt has acknowledged as an influence a liberating incident in Doris Lessing's *The Summer before the Dark* (1973). Lessing's Kate Brown, wife and mother, entering uncharted territory in her married life at the age of 45, undergoes a temporary mental crisis. Recovering, Kate is walking along a London street one evening after the pubs have closed, and feels unable to pass what she perceives as a few 'threatening' groups of young men. However, she forces herself to do so: 'No-one took any notice. [Kate] received indifferent glances, which turned off her at once, in search of stimulus. . . . [S]he might have been invisible'.[1]

In both kinds of manifestation, however, it is not just the fact that the menopause – more than any other event in a woman's life – can bring about marginalization that intrigues Byatt: she is unusual in giving her women, with an explicitness absent from Lessing's Kate Brown, their own voices. Those voices range through acquiescence, sardonic acceptance, rage, and comedy, as we may see in the case of *Possession*. Their depiction characterizes a number of the recent short stories, too, and we will look briefly at the protagonists of 'Medusa's Ankles' and 'The Djinn in the Nightingale's Eye'. As we have seen, Byatt, like Iris Murdoch, is uneasy with feminism as a dogma. Interviewed by Nicolas Tredell in May 1990, she turned to her sense of Maud Bailey's dilemma in *Possession*: 'I think Maud does hold her feminist views, but she hasn't solved, by holding them, the problem of how to behave, and she hasn't, which I think is purely comic, solved the problem of being very beautiful' (NT 60).

Several of the characters in *Possession* – Beatrice Nest and Val (who is given no last name) among the modern scholars, Christabel LaMotte and Blanche Glover, and (at the end of her life) even Ellen Ash, among their nineteenth-century originals – express thoughts on their marginality. Beatrice Nest, for instance, is introduced as follows:

> If people thought of Beatrice Nest – and not many did, not very often – it was her external presence, not her inner life that engaged their imagination. She was indisputably solid, and nevertheless amorphous, a woman of wide and abundant flesh, sedentary swelling hips, a mass of bosom, above which spread a cheerful-shaped face, crowned by a kind of angora hat, or thick wool-skein of crimped white hair, woven and tucked into a roll from which lost strands trailed and wandered in all directions. (*P.* 112)

The external presence does, all the same, breed fantasies that bear on the inner life: to Mortimer Cropper she resembles '[Lewis] Carroll's obstructive white sheep', to James Blackadder she is unhealthily and whitely arachnid (an interesting proleptic variation on Eugenia Alabaster in *Angels and Insects*), and to radical feminist scholarship in general 'some kind of guardian octopus, an ocean Fafnir, curled torpidly around her horde, putting up opaque screens of ink or watery smoke to obscure her whereabouts'. 'Sedentary' is the modifier common to all these perceptions. Beatrice Nest is, in short, a physical and ideological obstacle, an irrelevance to contemporary scholarship, as she pursues her endless task of editing the papers of Ellen

Ash (with whose nineteenth-century polymath husband R. H. Ash she had fallen in love as an undergraduate during 1938–41, a period of unprecedented liberation for women students).

Drawn initially to these papers by her passion for the man for whom Ellen Ash is 'helpmeet' rather than by any intrinsic interest in the particularity of her subject, Beatrice Nest nevertheless gradually becomes 'implicated' in a life that assumes its own importance, so that 'a kind of defensiveness rose up in her when Blackadder suggested Ellen was not the most suitable partner for a man so intensely curious about all possible forms of life. She became aware of the mystery of privacy . . .' (P. 115).

Meanwhile, Beatrice is perceived by her students in the 1950s and 1960s as 'motherly' and, later, in the more radical period that follows, as: 'lesbian, even . . . a repressed and unregenerate lesbian. In fact her thoughts about her own sexuality were dominated entirely by her sense of the massive, unacceptable bulk of her breasts' (P. 116).

Sensing 'her growing irrelevance to the deliberations of her department', Beatrice has taken early retirement, and is now stalled on the papers of Ellen Ash. She appears not to realize that 'the massive, unacceptable bulk of her breasts' could challenge a woman of different temperamental inclinations, such as Leonora Stern, to make another kind of statement about them, but she is capable of articulating her frustration to Maud Bailey, a member of a generation of scholars whose intellectual passions she can only dimly discern. She is, and (we are to assume) will remain, 'unreconstructed', but she is all the same aware of the issues involved.

> 'I expect you think I've very little to show for all these years of work on these papers. . . . I've felt very conscious of that – that slowness – with the increasing interest shown by – your sort of scholar – people with ideas about Ellen Ash and her work. All I had was a sort of sympathy for the – helpmeet aspect of her – and to be truthful, Dr Bailey, a real admiration for him, for Randolph Ash. *They* said it would be better to – to do this task which presented itself so to speak and seemed appropriate to my – my sex – my capacities as they were thought to be, whatever they were. A good feminist in *those* days, Dr Bailey, would have insisted on being allowed to work on the Ask and Embla poems.'
>
> 'Being allowed?'

57

'Oh. I see. Yes. On *working* on the Ask and Embla poems.' She hesitated. Then: 'I don't think you can imagine, Miss Bailey, how it was then. We were dependent and excluded persons. In my early days – indeed until the late 1960s – women were *not permitted* to enter the main Senior Common Room at Prince Albert College. . . . We thought it was bad being young . . . but it was worse when we grew older. There is an age at which, I profoundly believe, one becomes a *witch* . . .' (*P.* 220–1)

(Maud is, to Beatrice, 'Dr' in her professional capacity, but 'Miss' (and very much not 'Ms') on the personal level.)

In the scene prior to the final wrong-footing twist (the last scene in which the twentieth-century scholars have the chance to speak for themselves), Christabel's moving letter to Ash is discovered with his remains. Significantly it is Beatrice for whom the marginality of both wife and female lover, or (as Beatrice would doubtless say) 'mistress', to the community in which they have coexisted with Ash assumes the greatest poignancy:

Beatrice Nest was in tears. They rose to her eyes and flashed and fell. Maud put out a hand.

'Beatrice – '

'I'm sorry to be so silly. It's just so terrible to think – he can't ever have read it, can he? She wrote all that for no-one. She must have waited for an answer – and none can have come – '
(*P.* 503–4)

The figure of the witch, used by Beatrice of herself to Maud, occurs elsewhere in *Possession*. We encounter it in the early description of Roland's and Val's landlady, 'an octogenarian Mrs Irving', who 'had enticed them in like an old witch, Val said, by talking volubly to them in the garden about the quietness of the place, giving them each a small, gold, furry apricot from the espaliered trees along the curving brick wall' (*P.* 17). The Hansel and Gretel allusion is unavoidable. But we are most likely to be struck by an effect that Byatt uses to remarkable effect elsewhere in *Possession*, and that is the resonance with which a particular word transcends the two historical periods in which the novel is set. Those periods pivot around the word in question.

The poignancy of Beatrice's perception of that last unread letter of Christabel to Randolph obscures our knowledge of what we may ourselves hear, which is a disconcerting echo of those earlier words of Beatrice to Maud (although of course those of Christabel historically predate Beatrice's). Christabel writes her letter:

> *Oh, my dear, here I sit, an old witch in a turret, writing my verses by licence of my boorish brother-in-law, a* hanger on *as I had never meant to be, of my sister's good fortune (in the pecuniary sense) and I write to you, as if it was yesterday, of all that rage like iron bands burning round my breast, of the spite and the love (for you, for my sweet Maia, for poor Blanche too). But it is not yesterday, and you are very ill. (P. 500)*

Another instance of this backward recall arrestingly unites Val (who in a Murdochian touch (see EW 87) is liberated from Roland into a relationship with the solicitor Euan McIntyre) and Blanche Glover (the companion whom Christabel apparently abandons for Randolph and – finally – solitude). Whereas Christabel's perception of her eldritch status is far sharper than Beatrice's, the association we are invited to make between Val and Blanche gives each a voice of much more equal strength (and prepares us for the resourceful self-knowledge of Susannah in 'Medusa's Ankles' and Gillian Perholt in 'The Djinn in the Nightingale's Eye'). Prior to their final sterile break-up, Val remarks to Roland: 'I'm a superfluous person' (P. 218). Some pages later, Maud (unaware, unlike *Possession*'s readers, of Val's remark) rereads Blanche's suicide note.

Blanche's journal has earlier intimated that she has been rescued by Christabel from a life of endless governessing posts (we may think of Charlotte Brontë's Lucy Snowe in *Villette* (1853), a novel intriguingly discussed by Byatt and Sodré in *Imagining Characters*). Initially relieved and even elated to have been able to set up house together in Putney, the women drift apart. Blanche begins to intercept and destroy Randolph's letters to Christabel. Blanche's suicide note concludes: 'It has indeed been borne in upon me that here I am a superfluous creature. There I shall know and be known' (P. 309). What proved tragically fatal to Blanche enables Val comically to escape. Yet the apparent absoluteness of the contrast may also conceal a parallel between the two cases, linked as they are by the word 'superfluous'. Blanche has no choice but to leave this life for what she believes to be a spirit world 'on the other side'. This enables Blanche's construction as an existential human being with faith in a hereafter in which her 'capacities – great and here unwanted and unused' can be employed 'for love and for creative Work' (*P.* 309). Val, who, we are told, has beautiful ankles (*P.* 14), is transformed and fulfilled, as she could never be with Roland, by her relationship with Euan. Whether or not Blanche's beliefs are shared by her twentieth-century reader, her very recuperation by and into the twentieth-century plot of *Possession* gives her a voice and a role 'on the other side' that, despairingly, in the nineteenth-century plot, Blanche believed herself not to be capable of having. There are ways in which marginalization can liberate those who experience it, yet (ironically and sometimes tragically) that liberation may not always be palpable to the sufferer.

In 'Medusa's Ankles', the first of *The Matisse Stories*, the classicist Susannah had once been Suzie, 'when . . . she had made love all day to an Italian student on a course in Perugia . . . [but w]hat was this to anyone now?' (*MS* 22–3) Susannah is due to receive a translator's award on TV and thus feels obliged to visit her hairdresser. She has been a client of Lucian's salon for some while, having originally been attracted to it because a reproduction of Matisse's *Le Nu Rose* (1935) hangs above the coat-rack. But the narcissistic and sexually ambivalent Lucian is not usually interested in what interests Susannah. After going through a marital crisis, Lucian has removed the Matisse and had the shop redecorated 'very fashionably in the latest colours, battleship-grey and maroon' (*MS* 15). Although Susannah dislikes the new scheme, she continues to have her hair done there.

In a finely judged pun we have learnt that '[Susannah] came to trust [Lucian] with her disintegration' (*MS* 7), but on the critical day he is overworked and passes her on to his assistant Deirdre, who completes the job. There are many scenes of strikingly carnivalesque (that is, bad social or violent physical) behaviour in public throughout Byatt's work. Yet few in the entire Byatt œuvre match this, apart possibly from Thor Eskelund's outbreak towards the end of *The Game* (pp. 185–7) or Paul-Zag Ottokar's pyromaniac assault on Frederica's books in *Babel Tower* (pp. 454–7), as Susannah confronts her Medusa-like image in Deirdre's mirror:

Rage rose in her, for the fat-ankled woman, like a red flood, up from her thighs across her chest, up her neck, it must flare like a flag in her face, but how to tell in this daft cruel grey light? Deirdre was rolling up curls, piling them up, who would have thought the old woman had so much hair on her head? Sausages and snail shells, grape clusters and twining coils. . . . 'It's horrible,' said Susannah. '*I look like a middle-aged woman with a hair-do.*' (*MS* 23–4)

Whereupon, in a passage of rhetorically deadpan and very funny description, Susannah makes her own aesthetic and political statement, and breaks the place up:

When she had finished – and she went on, she kept going, until there was nothing else to hurl, for she was already afraid of what must happen when she had finished – there was complete human silence in the salon. . . . It was a strange empty battlefield, full of glittering fragments and sweet-smelling rivulets and puddles of venous-blue and fuchsia-red unguents, patches of crimson-streaked foam and odd intense spills of orange henna or cobalt and copper. (*MS* 26)

Lucian is surprisingly unperturbed ('The insurance'll pay. Don't worry. . . . You've done me a good turn in a way. It wasn't quite right, the colours' (*MS* 27)), and Susannah returns home intending to wash out her Medusa curls. But her husband, nameless, relegated to the footnotes of the story, returns early and unexpectedly:

She looked up at him speechless. He saw her. (Usually he did not.)
'You look different. You've had your hair done. I like it. It's lovely. It takes twenty years off you. You should have it done more often.'
And he came over and kissed her on the shorn nape of her neck, quite as he used to do. (*MS* 28)

The narratologist Gillian Perholt is involved in a far larger and more complex narrative of her own: the title-story takes up almost two-thirds of the entire volume of *The Djinn in the Nightingale's Eye*. Let us note – in conclusion – the nature of Gillian's first wish and its fulfilment, concentrating on the sense of comedy that arises from the juxtaposition of realism and magic. The djinn appears during the live transmission in Gillian's hotel room of a tennis match between Boris Becker and Henri Leconte.

The djinn frowned.

'I am a djinn of some power,' he said. 'I begin to find out how these emanations travel. Would you like a homunculus of your own?'

'I have three wishes,' said Dr Perholt cautiously. 'I do not want to expend one of them on the possession of a tennis-player.' (*DNE* 197)

The djinn nevertheless conjures a diminutive Becker into the hotel room before, at Gillian's urgent request, returning him to Monte Carlo, whereupon he collapses on court and withdraws temporarily from the match.

'They will not be able to continue,' said Gillian crossly, and then put her hand to her mouth in amazement, that a woman with a live djinn on her bed should still be interested in the outcome of a tennis match, only part of which she had seen. (*DNE* 200)

Gillian's first wish movingly illustrates her own sense of dignity in the face of the kind of future (even though a liberating one) that might await a Kate Brown. The djinn warns Gillian that the fulfilment of her wish 'cannot delay [her] Fate', and reveals his Otherness in the face of a society that would marginalize her (' "Amplitude, Madame, is desirable." "Not in my culture." '). And so Gillian, living in that culture but privileged to share what the djinn will reveal about his own, makes her first wish: 'I wish,' said Gillian, 'for my body to be as it was when I last really *liked* it, if you can do that' (*DNE* 201).

The djinn's Otherness is used by Byatt to enhance the comedy. While Gillian is incredulously examining her body in the bathroom, the djinn has been perusing the usual hotel literature, which includes a Gideon Bible. His English having been 'absorbed . . . by some kind of cerebral osmosis' (*DNE* 203), he quotes a passage that is, in its application to Gillian, preposterously disjunctive. The comic effect is heightened further by the djinn's readerly status as a *tabula rasa*, unaware (as he must be) of the passage's context, even though in previous eras he claims to have 'consorted . . . with the Queen of Sheba herself' (*DNE* 204): 'Who is she that looketh forth as the morning, fair as the moon, clear as the sun, and terrible as an army with banners?' (*DNE* 203).

9

'Language our Straitjacket': Violence, Enclosure, and Babble

Babel Tower offers three openings that correspond to the three main strands of its story, prefaced by a fourth that provides a kind of continuo. These alternative beginnings are of organic importance to both the book's form and content, for they initiate an interwoven, braided structure. That structure can be figured as a helix or spiral of arbitrary length which, when imagined vertically, assists in our understanding of the book's title.

The three postulated beginnings focus on Frederica Potter, on Daniel Orton, and on something new to the sequence, a narrative within the story, 'the book that was to cause so much trouble, but was then only scribbled heaps of notes, and a swarm of scenes, imagined and re-imagined' (*BT* 10), which will come to be called *Babbletower*. The continuo introduces not only the novel *Babel Tower* itself but the theme of sounds and visual characters, pertaining to a natural world under threat or to past civilizations now vanished, that are devoid of meaning – or at least of anything we could give significance to. Residual crackle or babble, they may be analogous to what Big Bang theorists would term 'black-body background radiation', but this is in no way to suggest they do not have their own beauty: 'The thrush sings his limited lovely notes. He stands on the stone, which we call his anvil or altar, and repeats his song. Why does his song give us such pleasure?' (*BT* 1).

The intermittent continuo will focus on the existence in the world of *Babel Tower* of a marginalized but now rehabilitated Marcus Potter. Marcus, now Dr Potter, is inscrutably involved with two sisters, one of whom is also – and unavailingly – involved both professionally and personally with a part-Danish geneticist investigating 'Darwinian selection in action' (*BT* 356). The project involves 'reading' the language of DNA on the backs of local snail populations, and one finding is that the pesticides whose entry into the food chain began to be a matter of public concern in the 1960s are effecting genetic changes 'as surely as radiation does' (*BT* 356). One of the decade's most influential ecological polemics, Rachel Carson's *Silent Spring*, confronted its readers with man's complicity in the threat of extinction to babble in the natural world.

The braiding together of *Babel Tower*'s three main plaited strands marks a new development in Byatt's writing. We have seen that she is constantly alive to the work performed by metaphor ('the figure of speech for carrying one idea into another' (*AI* 132)) in relating portrayals of different orders of reality to each other: the articulate expression of thought is doomed to a constant struggle with the deforming pressures of articulacy. In *Babel Tower* the *dangers* intrinsic to this struggle are put before us with an intensity we have not yet seen in Byatt's work. If there is one overriding theme in the book, a theme echoed in *Babbletower,* it is the very complexity of the area in which the battle is fought, the battle to maintain one's own inherent existential identity in the face of attempts by other forces to appropriate that identity away from one's own conception of it. This theme is examined through debates characteristic of the 1960s, such as those concerning the ethics of education, censorship, and parenting. It is also, at a level to which these debates may be thought ancillary, illustrated by the various disfiguring roles language itself plays within the working out of the plot of *Babel Tower*. Language guards against the violent frustration that must explode when articulacy either comes under threat, or simply cannot be achieved (as in the world of Nigel Reiver). Language can be used as a mask. Frederica tries to write a series of 'Laminations' to try to bridge the gap between reality and the words we use to describe it; if, at its trial for obscenity, *Babbletower* has already been found to be a work with 'a tendency to deprave and corrupt', is to resort to the argument of literary merit – as English law made possible during the 1960s – a possible counter-defence? And language operates (in an idea Iris Murdoch plays with in her first published novel) as a net 'made by words which do not describe what [one] feels is happening' (*BT* 324). Byatt has long been attracted to Murdoch's view that 'reality . . . "is more, and other, than our descriptions of it" ' (*DF* 11). These aspects of one enormous problem – specified above as recourse to physical violence where language is perceived as inadequate, and language as masquerade and net – might be thought of as the most recurrent manifestations of the field on which, in *Babel Tower*, the battle against the distortion of narrative is fought. Late in the book Frederica reflects on the predicament facing those whose actions come under judicial scrutiny, who 'have been made to recite travesties of their life stories, in language they would never have chosen for themselves' (*BT* 595).

Let us approach them by way of one of the ancillary debates, that concerning the ethics of parenting. *Babel Tower* is set in the period 1964–7. *Still Life* left off six years previously, with the death of Stephanie Orton *née* Potter. As we pursue the strands of *Babel Tower*, we discover that Daniel, Stephanie's widower, has abandoned his children, Will and Mary, and – in significant measure – his faith. Will and Mary are under the guardianship of their grandparents Bill and Winifred Potter, while Daniel, in London, operates a telephone helpline from the crypt of a disused City church with the help of a small group of co-workers. Frederica is trapped in an unhappy marriage to Nigel Reiver, the ship-owning county squire of an estate in Hereford-shire. The couple have a small son, Leo. Leo and his cousins Will and Mary have never met; Frederica has cut herself off from her parents.

The reactions of Daniel and Frederica have arisen out of a primal need to survive. The loss of a wife and a sister seems to have forced each into different yet comparable postures of survival that contrast with the more steadfast attitudes of Stephanie's parents, whose grief is nevertheless undeniable. Daniel's desertion of his children has scarred Will (who, as has been intimated in *Still Life*, is not to survive long into adult-hood; see also *BT* 241) yet enabled Mary to adapt to her situation more equably. These responses are to be thought of as of the same order of inexplicability as the very genetic make-up of the children themselves. The action of *Babel Tower*, which is related in the present tense throughout, is perceived through Frederica's consciousness more than those of any of the book's other characters, and so allows us many glimpses of the disarmingly precocious Leo. Leo's speech patterns modulate during the book in ways that reflect his changing circumstances, and emphasize his vulnerability. When Frederica makes her melodramatic romanticized night-time escape from her husband's Bran House, the sinister Bluebeard's Castle that has been in the Reiver family for several generations, it is the 5-year-old Leo who actively seeks her out and clings to her (rather than the other way around), insisting on accompanying her to London. The rendezvous arranged with Frederica's rescuers and former Cambridge friends does not quite go according to plan:

> 'Hullo, Leo,' says Alan gravely. 'Are you coming with us?'
>
> The boy cannot answer.
>
> Frederica says, 'He took matters into his own hands. Can he come?'
>
> 'I don't think you can be separated,' says Alan judiciously. (*BT* 129)

The novel will force us to examine what motherhood is: is it the conventionally civilized understanding of the provision of loving or at least affectionate care, nourishment, and shelter as portrayed by the jealous surrogate, the Reivers' housekeeper Pippy Mammott; or is it beyond reason, more intense, more atavistic? In London, Frederica encounters other forms of parenting that help her give language to her schizoid sense of being physically fused with Leo. Moving in temporarily and chastely with Thomas Poole, himself the abandoned father of four children, one of whom, Simon Vincent, is almost certainly the son of Alexander Wedderburn (something neither Frederica nor Thomas nor, indeed, the boy himself is to know), Frederica watches Leo develop interactive skills with other children. At the same time she is ambivalent about the consequences for her relationship with him. Later, also at Alexander's behest, Frederica will share a house with her age-peer, the unmarried Agatha Mond, and her daughter Saskia. There are hints (*BT* 360–4, 401) that the mystery of Saskia's paternity – is she related to Leo? – will be revealed later in the *roman fleuve*. At any rate, Agatha Mond has been able to rise to a position of seniority in the British Civil Service because of its surprisingly humane provision for 'up to three illegitimate children, with maternity leave, and no questions asked' (*BT* 170).

It is Stephanie's death that has confronted Frederica and Daniel, in their different ways, with the ethics of parenting. One reason for Daniel's escape to London is that he has been, and continues to be, traumatized by a vision of his wife's dead face. He is also unwilling to see her brother Marcus:

> who was in the room when the sparrow fled under the refrigerator and the refrigerator struck. Daniel has never asked whether, if Marcus had shown more presence of mind, he could have saved her. He is afraid of his own rage. . . . Marcus does not want to see Daniel. Partly for Daniel's reasons. . . . Marcus knows that he is guilty of Stephanie's death. He knows that the one person – apart from the dead – whom he has mortally hurt is Daniel, though he knows also that irremediable harm has been done to Will and Mary . . . He does not think of Frederica as someone wounded by what has happened. (*BT* 52–4)

In this Marcus is mistaken, for at the time of Stephanie's death none of Frederica's friends, encountered earlier in the sequence, appears to have been capable of helping her. The only person able to offer sufficient consolation is Nigel Reiver. It is on the basis of this consolation, and on what Frederica will later troublingly admit has been an admixture of good sexual chemistry, that Nigel and Frederica have embarked on their marriage. During the divorce hearing, Frederica describes their early relationship: 'It was the attraction of opposites. I didn't know anything about him. He seemed – you [Nigel's Counsel] quoted it – *other*. I liked that. I thought he was more – more self-sufficient and grown-up, than most of the men I knew' (*BT* 491–2). Stephanie's death has taken away from both Daniel and Frederica any saving power that language might have had. This in turn has thrown them into their present predicaments. Marcus believes that Will and Mary have had 'irremediable harm' done to them as a result of Daniel's predicament; what Marcus does not understand is that Leo's very existence, coupled with his eerie intuitiveness and its effect on his mother, is actually *attributable* to Frederica's predicament.

The opposite to which Frederica has been attracted is not a

simple one: that is, Nigel's self-sufficiency and maturity, his being good in bed, are only part of a fuller personality she comes to discover as the marriage progresses. The Potters are a bookish, atheist-humanist, politically left-wing, and also financially modest family; the Reivers are a culturally philistine, ostensibly church-going, true-blue Conservative and county family – these terms are used not pejoratively so much as to indicate what the Potters are not. The Reivers also lack imagination, and, because they are culturally impoverished, they are less articulate than Frederica. Again, this is not to make a judgement so much as to point up the fuller consequences of the 'otherness' to which Frederica was originally attracted. Only when it is too late does Frederica discover that Nigel is also a tyrannical and physically violent husband: that is, violence takes the place of reasoned articulacy because Nigel seems incapable of the latter.

Babel Tower's portrayal of the marriage is saved from banality by a narrative sophistication that we may think of as operating fantastically. Although it is Frederica's consciousness through which the entire marriage is perceived, Byatt manages as narrator to distance herself unfathomably from undivided sympathy with Frederica's values, which we cannot but assume are closer to her own than are those of the Reivers. (One suspects that the fantastic effect is partly gained by the use of the present tense in the narrative of *Babel Tower*.)

The narrator controls our view of Frederica as a wonder-tale *princesse lointaine* in Bran House in a deceptively deadpan manner. She becomes a prisoner in it: when her friends write to her, their letters are intercepted; when they visit her, they are rebuffed with impeccable English county manners laced with a quasi-sinister venom; when they attempt to telephone her, the surrogate stepmother Pippy Mammott dissemblingly puts them off. The household closes ranks, even when evidence of physical violence, such as a smashed-up bloodstained bedroom, becomes manifest. Yet, somehow, we cannot wholeheartedly sympathize with Frederica herself, even though we may feel repelled by the circumstances she becomes drawn into. Attempting while alone in the house to find some possibly purloined letters, Frederica discovers a set of keys. These enhance the Bluebeard motif: one opens a suitcase that gives off . . . an odour of decay like ripe cheese. It turns out to contain a wad of clearly unwashed rugger clothing in various colours – tangerine and black, a sumptuous purple and crimson. There are socks with what she supposes to be ancient mud, liquid in the 1950s, even, caked dust since then – she has never known Nigel play rugger. She locks it again quickly. (*BT* 100)

Another of Nigel's suitcases (later in the novel to be referred to as 'Bluebeard's cupboard') contains a collection of violent and degrading pornography (I use the adjectives as objectively as I can). Frederica, sophisticated, liberal, and sexually experienced as she is, is surprised by the revulsion this discovery evokes in her. Although her abhorrence is believable at the time, we can also share the scepticism voiced by Nigel's Counsel during the divorce hearing as to whether this response is not primarily a pretext for her allegations of adultery and cruelty. The entire episode is woven into the use of obscene language as a mask for what may – under the provisions of the 1959 Obscene Publications Act – be redeeming literary merit. Again the ethics of parenting are involved here. Frederica is never one to censor Leo's reading, but it is clear that she prefers J. R. R. Tolkien's *The Hobbit* to Beatrix Potter's *The Tale of Mr Tod* to which Leo (who has inherited his genes from both Frederica and Nigel) returns again and again. Is this innocent pleasure in the childishly unpleasant, or does it reinforce the strong emphasis on the olfactory senses, specifically on stench and stink in *Babel Tower*?

> 'I will bury that nasty person in the hole which he has dug. I will bring my bedding out, and dry it in the sun,' said Mr Tod.
> 'I will get soft soap, and monkey soap, and all sorts of soap; and soda and scrubbing brushes; and persian powder; and carbolic to remove the smell. I must have a disinfecting. Perhaps I may have to burn sulphur.' (*BT* 104)

In certain very specific ways this passage prepares us for the malodorousness of Jude Mason (who on his own admission emits 'a very ancient and fish-like smell'), but here it is more significant still that it is Leo's olfactory acuity that forces Frederica to realize that 'She has failed a test she was waiting for' when she mistakes John Ottokar for his twin brother Paul (*BT* 406), whose odour is offensive to Leo.

Frederica's articulate response to the threat to her inherent existential selfhood is to pursue the idea of what she thinks of as layered or cumulative 'lamination' (*VG* 274–5). In *The Virgin in the Garden*, lamination had been an abstract theoretical concern that she now recalls in *Babel Tower*:

> she, Frederica, had had a vision of being able to be all the things she was: language, sex, friendship, thought, just as long as these were kept scrupulously separate, *laminated*, like geological strata, not seeping and flowing into each other like organic cells boiling to join and divide and join in a seething Oneness. Things were best cool, and clear, and fragmented, if fragmented was what they were. (*BT* 312)

Her experimental work *Laminations* begins to develop in the form of an aleatory William Burroughs-like cut-out of a letter from Nigel's solicitors concerning provisions for Leo's welfare ('that you arrange immediately to Brock's preparatory intermediate care for the boy, parents will be free to earn money part-time. His request is both kinds. My client does not care for the boy and he hopes that you in the interests of his son ... [*sic*]' (*BT* 378)). She does the same with passages from Lawrence and Forster that are among the books on the extramural course she is giving. She adds extracts from Thomas Mann, R. D. Laing, Nietzsche, a Beat Poet manifesto, Beckett, Blake – and an anecdote of her own that begins to give form to experience; but Frederica gradually becomes dissatisfied with *Laminations* and abandons it.

Babbletower is a more successful masquerade, even though it falls foul of the 1959 Obscene Publications Act. In a post-*Lady Chatterley* trial that may possibly be drawing on the proceedings against Hubert Selby's *Last Exit to Brooklyn* in 1968, the author and publishers are convicted (the trial is reported in great detail), only to be acquitted on a technicality when they appeal (the acquittal is reported as a newspaper headline almost at the end of the book). Setting the trial in 1965 allows it to impact on the Ian Brady and Myra Hindley 'Moors Murders' hearings, which are beginning just as capital punishment is being abolished in Britain. The account of the *Babbletower* trial is a marvellously controlled instance of the way in which legal language both obfuscates and renders down the particularity of a narrative that claims literary status – and *Babel*

Tower enhances the literary status of *Babbletower* and its genesis in a variety of ways.

When we first encounter Daniel, his telephone helpline is victimized by a disturbed but clearly intelligent caller who comes to be known as Steelwire. He possesses a blasphemous rhetoric and a distasteful though well-bred speaking voice that will later be labelled 'sawing'. There is a moment of classic anagnorisis or recognition when Daniel, visiting the art school where Frederica is teaching, and Steelwire, alias Jude Mason, who is modelling there, encounter each other corporeally for the first time; and a later such moment (rather less surprising) when we learn that Jude Mason is none other than the author of *Babbletower*. The extracts we are given from *Babbletower* certainly contain material, derived from Sade and the gentler more eccentric Charles Fourier, that some would consider obscene, or at least distressing. But there is incontestably much that is not of this nature. The literary defence of *Babbletower* seems centred on its generic provenance: it portrays a Utopia to which a small group of people, escaping the French Revolutionary Terror, journey and in which they take refuge. Under their leader Culvert and his partner Lady Roseace, it is proposed that all rules and constraints be done away with. Incidentally it is Agnes Mond who, viewing cover designs for *Babbletower* produced by the art-school students, sees what no one else does as she admires

> a tomato-coloured double-apple-cheeked fruit, with a serpentine pointed conical tube in very bright green, coiled round it and penetrating it. . . . 'It's a good joke,' says Agatha, in her mild, dark voice. 'Cul-vert. Rose-Arse. It's all there, in *purely visual language*.' (*BT* 440)

Yet consideration of genre leads, as any reasonably experienced reader might be expected to guess, to the Dostoevskian dictum 'do as thou wilt shall be the whole of the law' (*BT* 7).

The experienced reader will also register that, because the extracts from *Babbletower* are embedded in *Babel Tower*, connections might be expected, and indeed cannot be avoided. Thus La Tour Bruyarde becomes a fantastic version of Bran House, each in it own way impregnable; the psychopomp Culvert becomes a fantastic version of the dominant Nigel Reiver; and Lady Roseace's tiring of the *Babbletower* Utopia and attempting to escape figures Frederica's ill-fated attempts to rid herself of

71

Nigel. But, of course, the parallels are not exact: it is more as though *Babbletower*, its world, and the issues it raises provide a prattling commentary on the worlds inhabited by and issues facing the other characters in the braided construct that makes up *Babel Tower*. Sometimes the strands are twined together particularly closely, as when, during the obscenity trial, it becomes clear that it is possible to read *Babbletower* as a *roman à clef* on the debaucheries formerly practised at the Cumberland public school Swineburn, which it turns out Jude Mason and his defending Counsel have attended, and for which Leo Reiver has been put down because his father went there.

The inexactness of the parallels raises a larger point that has informed Byatt's novel-writing from the very beginning, which is that (like Iris Murdoch) Byatt explores the battle between 'real people' and 'images' in ways that involve intense scrutiny of the inadequacy of 'either/or' readings of symbolic language. After the divorce hearing Frederica has a particularly bizarre dream (*BT* 520–2), which blends the traumatic experiences of the hearing with her role as the virgin princess Elizabeth in *Astraea*. She enters a garden filled with 'great cats', sensing that, if she can reach the stone lion at the other end, all will be well. We may decode this sense as Frederica's fear that she may not be awarded custody of Leo. Frederica manages to reach and 'fall' on the lion, at which point she awakes, but she has been pursued by three predators, who may represent the Reiver sisters and Pippy Mammott – three surrogate mothers recalling the security of Bran House. But Nigel's solicitor is named Guy Tiger, while his colleague is called Laurence Ounce. The feline associations of these adversarial names (brilliantly unobtrusive in the latter case), and the leonine associations of her son's, combine with the threat of surrogate motherhood to create a dream-world which is full of predators, both 'good' and 'bad'. The effect is that it is impossible, both for Frederica and for us as readers, to 'separate out' Leo, whom Frederica loves, passionately and atavistically, from the hostility by which Frederica is surrounded. The symbolism (as in Spenser) is complex precisely because it resists reductive reading.

The clearest description of language as a net in *Babel Tower* is provided by the narrator through Frederica's consciousness, and with it this account of the novel may fittingly conclude:

Frederica sees herself as a caged or netted beast. She sees something limp and snarling in a barred cage on wheels, in a hunter's net suspended from a bough. The net is not made by Nigel, who ran after her, panting, in hot blood, and hurled an axe at her, letting her own blood out of her haunch. The net is made by words which do not describe what she feels is happening: adultery, connivance, pre-nuptial incontinence, petitioner, respondent. She tries to think out these words. Adultery has connotations of impurity (adulterated butter, adulterated white flour) or perhaps of theft? Incontinence somehow equates sexual pleasure with lack of muscular control of bowels or bladder: *the proper use of the sphincter is to contain*, thinks Frederica. These legal words carry with them the whole history of a society in which a woman was a man's property, and also a part of his flesh, not to be contaminated. And behind continence and incontinence is the alien, ancient, and powerful history of Christian morals. (*BT* 324)

10

Conclusion:
The Fantastic Vein

Looking back over Byatt's work we may detect an interestingly self-conscious critiquing of her own artistry as early as *The Game*. The best-selling novelist Julia Corbett obsessively recalls a newspaper review of her work:

> 'In Miss Julia Corbett's first two novels an element of romantic fantasy was uneasily blended with a warm, human understanding of very real daily problems. In her later work she has consolidated her achievement in the second field – she is probably the best of that increasing number of women writers who explore in loving detail the lives of those trapped in comfort by washing-machines and small children – but with the fantastic romantic overtones some of the vigour has been lost. In the earlier books, clumsily conveyed, was a sense of possibilities and concerns outside domestic claustrophobia. I sometimes wish Miss Corbett could see her way to reopening, reinvigorating her fantastic vein; she might then have it in her to be a very good writer.' (*G.* 47)

The argument of this brief conclusion is that the abandonment of 'fantastic romantic overtones' and the closure of the 'fantastic vein' discerned in Julia Corbett's fiction represent a path Byatt's own fiction has not taken. Instead a sense of the fantastic has enhanced Byatt's continued interest in the lives of women, men, and children, and her long-held conviction (shared with Iris Murdoch though expressed very differently) that the novel represents a struggle between 'real people' and 'images'. What forms has this enhancement taken? It is possible to distil at least three from the preceding account of Byatt's work.

First, there is the language through which Byatt's characters express themselves. What I want to stress here is not so much the determined attempt to give each character her or his own language or idiolect, but some of the ways in which those idiolects can work unpredictably or even bizarrely, thwarting or second-guessing any preconceptions the reader might wish to entertain about those characters. This unpredictability is not consistent – the novelist retains her freedom to deploy it when and where she will – but when it does occur it is invariably striking and quite often humorous. It tends to occur with characters who are perceived or who perceive themselves as marginal. The example of Val in *Possession* may serve as an illustration:

> [Val] acquired an IBM golfball typewriter and did academic typing at home in the evenings and various well-paid temping jobs during the day. She worked in the City and in teaching hospitals, in shipping firms and art galleries. She resisted pressure to specialise. She would not be drawn out to talk about her work, to which she almost never referred without the adjective 'menial'. 'I must do just a few more menial things before I go to bed' or, more oddly, 'I was nearly run over on my menial way this morning.' (P. 13–14)

It is the 'more oddly' that allows the narrator scope in her description of the two Vals, one who leads a subterranean ill-dressed existence in the basement flat, and one ('This mournfully bright menial Val') who presents herself to the professional world in and for which she works. The degree to which the narrator is showing sympathy to Val's self-estimation is not really the point. It is more as though the reader is being given the chance to watch the narrator's inscrutability at work.

This is not, of course, to say that the narrator lays all her characters bare, or walks in and out and through their psyches with no restraint whatever. It is rather to suggest that she respects their thoughts, their self-estimates, and seems as unable as the reader is to discern what (in this case) is really meant by, or lies behind, Val's use of 'menial'. Val remains opaque, and this opacity is, it seems to me, commensurate with the fantastic vein that makes the author of *Possession* a better novelist than the author of *A Sense of Glory*.

This implies that the author who exercises a fantastic vein may, secondly, be selective in what she chooses to reveal about the inner lives of her characters. As narrator she has characteristic rhetorical tricks of her own: Fergus is dimly discerned by Roland in the British Library as 'something rapid and white and golden' (P. 32), and one could find many instances of similarly arresting perceptions elsewhere in the books. Fergus is one of the marginal characters in *Possession* about whom the narrator chooses not to reveal a great deal; Blackadder is another. In contrast, we know a great deal (as we have seen) about Beatrice's inner life and her own self-estimate. What Byatt is doing is very similar to what Ellen Ash does in her Journal: at one point Beatrice sees the purpose of this Journal in terms of 'bafflement', but towards the end of *Possession* we encounter Ellen herself for the first and last time:

> She put more coal and more pieces of wood on the fire, and made a brave little blaze, by the side of which she sat down to manufacture the carefully edited, the carefully *strained* (the metaphor was one of jelly-making) truth of her journal. She would decide later what to do with that. It was both a defence against, and a bait for, the gathering of ghouls and vultures. (P. 461–2)

We note, in passing, the domestication of the process in the jelly-making metaphor. The narrator acts, similarly, in respect (for instance) of Mortimer Cropper, whom we see in Soho: 'His own tastes were precise, narrow, and somewhat specialist' (P. 304). We are not told what they are, and the phrasing has a portentousness about it that seems at odds with the more banal sexual *frisson* we see him experiencing as a biographer, collector, even a fetishist and a thief. Again, and in a different way, Cropper is lent, through the tapping of the narrator's fantastic vein, an opacity that makes him what he is, not a stereotype but someone who is simultaneously 'a real person' and 'an image'.

Byatt's use of real people, thirdly, in the *roman fleuve*, is nothing if not bold and striking. Various of the period's Great and Good, such as Dr Roy Strong (art historian), Dames Sybil Thorndike (actress) and Helen Gardner (Renaissance scholar), Lady Longford (author), Dr Frances Yates (Renaissance scholar), and Lady Antonia Fraser (popular historian) are all present at the fictive showing in the National Portrait Gallery in 1968 that forms the prologue to *The Virgin in the Garden*. The Prince Albert College of *Possession*, a thinly disguised version of University College London, makes a brief reappearance in *Babel Tower*, along with a fictive academic who offers expert testimony in the *Babbletower* obscenity trial – as does Anthony Burgess. We saw earlier a similar use of real historical people in 'Precipice-Encurled' and 'The Conjugial Angel'. No contemporary English novelist so palpably blurs the distinction between *real* 'real people' and 'images'. This aspect of Byatt's fantastic vein casts fascinating light on the complex relationship between fact and fiction.

Towards the end of 1994, Professor Linda K. Hughes of Texas Christian University, Fort Worth, editor of *Victorian Poetry*, received, doubtless to her surprise, a letter from Dr Maud Michell-Bailey announcing the discovery of two hitherto unknown fragmentary poems by Christabel LaMotte. They had been found at Seal Court on the back of a drawing of the Winter Garden there, 'done by May, or Maia LaMotte'. Michell-Bailey considered the fragments of biographical interest. The first speculates on how 'In mockery of eternity' the speaker will be haunted by 'two angry spirits', one white (Michell-Bailey speculates that this may refer to Blanche Glover) and one grey (evidently Randolph Henry Ash). The second fragment focuses on LaMotte's perception of herself as a witch in a tower. Michell-Bailey's letter continues:

> What interests me ... particularly, in this poem, is the image of the thread as something binding the 'witch' to the 'small head' or 'gold head'. I have noticed this image of an elastic thread joining mother and child in other women's poetry about maternity – a kind of metaphoric post-umbilical cord, whose presence is experienced as a physical tug and limitation. I have indeed, experienced sensations of precisely this kind since the birth of my own daughter, Rowan, and have had dreams very like the images in this poem, before the discovery of the poem itself. Feminist criticism admits the validity of the personal response, so I can say that before the birth of my daughter I had quite failed to imagine the nature of the pain LaMotte must daily have experienced, seeing her child and being unable to acknowledge the tie – so literally, the tie.[1]

The two fragments, whose first lines are, respectively, 'When I shall come to my last home' and 'The witch is the bobbin', were subsequently published in *Victorian Poetry*.

Notes

CHAPTER 1. INTRODUCTION: GLOBAL WRITER, THINKING CHARACTERS

1. Charles Davy, 'A Game of Chess', in *Words in the Mind* (London: Chatto & Windus, 1965), 91–9.
2. Ibid. 94.
3. Christopher Hope and A. S. Byatt, *Contemporary Writers: A. S. Byatt* (London: Book Trust and British Council, 1990).

CHAPTER 2. DETACHED AUTONOMY: FATHERS, DAUGHTERS, AND SISTERS

1. Joanne V. Creighton, 'Sisterly Symbiosis: Margaret Drabble's *The Waterfall* and A. S. Byatt's *The Game*', *Mosaic*, 20/1 (Winter 1987), 15.
2. Olga Kenyon, *Women Novelists Today* (Brighton: Harvester, 1988). 57.
3. Jane Campbell, 'The Hunger of the Imagination in A. S. Byatt's *The Game*', *Critique*, 29 (1988), 160.
4. Virginia Woolf, *Between the Acts* (1941; Harmondsworth: Penguin, 1953), 72.
5. Kenyon, *Women Novelists*, 57.

CHAPTER 3. EROTIC POWER, ART, AND MYTH

1. Olga Kenyon, *Women Novelists Today* (Brighton: Harvester, 1988), 67–8.
2. Juliet Dusinberre, 'Forms of Reality in A. S. Byatt's *The Virgin in the Garden*', *Critique*, 24 (1982), 55–62.
3. Ibid. 59.

CHAPTER **4**. THE PRIVATE LIFE

1. Jean-Louis Chevalier, 'Conclusion in *Possession* by [A. S.] Byatt, in Lucien le Bouille (ed.), *Fins de romans: Aspects de la conclusion dans la littérature anglaise* (Caen: Presses Universitaires de Caen, 1993), 109–31.
2. Ibid. 117.
3. Ibid.
4. Jane Campbell, ' "This Somehow May be Thishow": Fact, Fiction, and Intertextuality in [A. S.] Byatt's "Precipice-Encurled" ', *Studies in Short Fiction*, 28/2 (Spring 1992), 120.
5. Ibid. 116.

CHAPTER **8**. 'VISIBLE BUT UNSEEN': MENOPAUSE AND MARGINALIZATION

1. Doris Lessing, *The Summer before the Dark* (New York: Knopf, 1973), 179.

CHAPTER **10**. CONCLUSION: THE FANTASTIC VEIN

1. Transcript provided by Gill Marsden.

Select Bibliography

WORKS BY A. S. BYATT

Fiction and Literary Criticism

Shadow of A Sun (London: Chatto & Windus, 1964). Reissued with an Introduction as *The Shadow of the Sun* (London: Vintage, 1991).

Degrees of Freedom: The Novels of Iris Murdoch (London: Chatto & Windus, 1965). Reissued with a Foreword and additional matter, including reviews of subsequent Murdoch novels, a digest of Byatt's 1976 British Council pamphlet (see below), and a selected primary and secondary bibliography as *Degrees of Freedom: The Early Novels of Iris Murdoch* (London: Vintage, 1994). Literary criticism.

The Game (London: Chatto & Windus, 1967; Penguin edn., 1983; London: Vintage, 1992).

Wordsworth and Coleridge in their Time (London: Nelson, 1970). Reissued as *Unruly Times: Wordsworth and Coleridge in their Time* (London: The Hogarth Press, 1989). Literary criticism.

Iris Murdoch (London: Longman, 1976). Literary criticism.

The Virgin in the Garden (London: Chatto & Windus, 1978; London: Vintage, 1994).

Ed., George Eliot, *The Mill on the Floss* (London: Penguin, 1979).

Still Life (London: Chatto & Windus, 1985; London: Vintage, 1995).

Sugar and Other Stories (London: Chatto & Windus, 1987; Penguin Books, 1988).

Possession: A Romance (London: Chatto & Windus, 1990; London: Vintage, 1991).

Ed. with Nicholas Warren, *George Eliot: Selected Essays, Poems and Other Writings* (Harmondsworth: Penguin Classics, 1990). Literary criticism.

Passions of the Mind: Selected Writings (London: Chatto & Windus, 1991; London: Vintage, 1993). Literary criticism, including previously uncollected material, ranging from the Introductions to the Penguin reprint of Elizabeth Bowen's *The House in Paris* and Virago's reissues of a number of Willa Cather's novels, to reviews and full-length articles on a variety of literary and painterly topics.

Angels and Insects (London: Chatto & Windus, 1992; London: Vintage, 1993).

'Reading, Writing, Studying: Some Questions about Changing Conditions for Writers and Readers', *Critical Quarterly*, 35/4 (Winter 1993) 3–7.

The Matisse Stories (London: Chatto & Windus, 1993; London: Vintage, 1994).

The Djinn in the Nightingale's Eye (London: Chatto & Windus, 1994; London: Vintage, 1995).

'The Great Green Worm', translation of Marie-Catherine D'Aulnoy's 'Le Serpentin vert' (1698), in Marina Warner (ed. & introd.), *Wonder Tales: Six Stories of Enchantment*, with illustrations by Sophie Herxheimer (London: Chatto & Windus, 1994), 189–229.

'A New Body of Writing: Darwin and Recent British Fiction', in A. S. Byatt and Alan Hollinghurst, eds, *New Writing 4* (London: Vintage in association with the British Council, 1995), 439–48. Literary criticism: presents a strongly argued case for what is best in the British fiction of the 1980s and 1990s.

With Ignês Sodré, *Imagining Characters: Six Conversations about Women Writers*, ed. Rebecca Swift (London: Chatto & Windus, 1995). The works treated are: Jane Austen, *Mansfield Park*; Charlotte Brontë, *Villette*; George Eliot, *Daniel Deronda*; Willa Cather, *The Professor's House*; Iris Murdoch, *An Unofficial Rose*; and Toni Morrison, *Beloved*.

'A Lamia in the Cevennes'. In Christopher Hope and Peter Porter, eds, *New Writing 5* (London: Vintage in association with the British Council, 1996), 1–17.

Babel Tower (London: Chatto & Windus, 1996).

Film

Angels and Insects (Samuel Goldwyn Co.: 1995), based on 'Morpho Eugenia', from A. S. Byatt's *Angels and Insects*. Starring Mark Rylance as William Adamson, Kristin Scott Thomas as Matty Crompton, Patsy Kensit as Eugenia Alabaster, Douglas Henshall as Edgar Alabaster. Screenplay by Belinda Haas and Philip Haas. Directed by Philip Haas.

Interviews

Chevalier, Jean-Louis, 'Entretien avec A. S. Byatt', in *Journal of the Short Story in English* (Presses de l'Université d'Angers), 22 (Summer 1994), 12–27. Disarming interview in English with Byatt's French translator, focusing on a variety of aspects of the shorter (and thus most recent) fiction.

Dusinberre, Juliet, interview published in Janet Todd (ed.), *Women Writers Talking* (New York: Holmes & Meier, 1983), 181–95. An informative and delicately managed conversation in which Byatt, speaking on educational matters, stresses the limits of her sympathy with women's studies programmes and literary feminism. On her own imagination: 'When I read I inhabit a world which is more real than the world in which I live, or perhaps I should say that I am more alive in it. It is a language world' (pp. 184–85).

Tredell, Nicolas, *Conversations with Critics* (Manchester: Carcanet, 1994), 58–74. First appeared in shortened form in *PN Review*, 77 (Jan.–Feb. 1991), 24–8. The most probing interview to date results from Tredell's thorough research, his intelligent questions, and his admirable gift of drawing out his interviewees without being intrusive. Presents Byatt in the first place as a thinker, with the practice of critical theory and feminism (about which she expresses articulate and persuasive reservations) as ancillary but significant.

Wachtel, Eleanor, *Writers & Company in Conversation with Eleanor Wachtel* (1993; San Diego, New York, and London: Harcourt Brace & Co, 1994), 77–89. Interview prepared in collaboration with Sandra Rabinovitch. Reveals that Byatt was originally called 'Susan', that the 'Antonia' arose at the behest of a schoolteacher directing a production of *The Tempest*, and that the form 'A. S.' attracted her as a *nom de plume* 'because it was nothing to do with the family and it sounded rather like T. S. Eliot' (p. 77).

[Only the most substantial interviews are listed here. A plethora of journalistic interviews and profiles was sparked by the success of *Possession* during the closing months of 1990 and – in the USA – early 1991.]

BIOGRAPHICAL AND CRITICAL STUDIES

Alexander, Flora, *Contemporary Women Novelists* (London: Arnold, 1989). Contains (pp. 34–40) a sound account of *Still Life* as the conclusion to a chapter entitled 'Versions of the Real'. Specifies Byatt's reservations about feminist approaches to literature.

—— 'A. S. Byatt', in Theo D'haen *et al.* (eds.), *Post-war Literatures in English: A Lexicon of Contemporary Authors*, 16 (June 1992), 1–10, A1–2, B1. A biographical and critical account of Byatt's achievement up to and including *Possession*.

Ashworth, Anne, 'Fairy Tales in A. S. Byatt's *Possession*', *Journal of Evolutionary Psychology*, 15/1–2 (March 1994), 93–4. Confines itself to the influence of the Brothers Grimm.

Campbell, Jane, 'The Hunger of the Imagination in A. S. Byatt's *The Game*', *Critique*, 29 (1988), 147–62. Fine account of the self-reflexiveness of *The Game*: 'When the characters ... try to imagine each other – and this is the central action of the book – the result must ... be failure' (P. 154).

—— ' "This Somehow May Be Thishow": Fact, Fiction, and Intertextuality in [A. S.] Byatt's "Precipice-Encurled" ', *Studies in Short Fiction*, 28/2 (Spring 1991), 115–23. A wonderfully rich and discerning essay on the complexity of 'Precipice-Encurled' that thoroughly earns its conclusion, that in this short story 'the language of incompleteness and shattering, like the structure, testifies to the failure of enclosure'.

Chevalier, Jean-Louis, 'Conclusion in *Possession* by [A. S.] Byatt', in Lucien le Bouille (ed.), *Fins de romans: Aspects de la conclusion dans la littérature anglaise* (Caen: Presses Universitaires de Caen, 1993), 109–31. An essay of intense verbal sensitivity in which 'conclusion' is considered both as trial and as coronation. Deals with the ethics of conclusion.

—— 'What Are Little Girls Made Of? Étude de "Sugar", de A. S. Byatt' [Congrès de la SAES, Besançon, 1989], *Les Années Trente* (Université de Nantes), 14 (June 1991), 1–13. Argues that 'Sugar' is neither a short story, nor an imaginary fable, nor yet a fictional text, but 'une réflexion sur la mesure de l'imaginaire dans les récits de vie' (p. 2).

Creighton, Joanne V., 'Sisterly Symbiosis: Margaret Drabble's *The Waterfall* and A. S. Byatt's *The Game*', *Mosaic*, 20/1 (Winter 1987), 15–29. Quixotic but unconvincing psychobiographical attempt '[to] explore the extent to which the lives of Byatt and Drabble illustrate how female identity and creativity are complicated and enriched by a sisterly "other" '. Explicitly resists endorsement from either writer – indeed admits it draws 'protests to the contrary' (p. 24) – and fails to provide other than circumstantial evidence.

Dusinberre, Juliet, 'Forms of Reality in A. S. Byatt's *The Virgin in the Garden*', *Critique*, 24 (1982), 55–62. Accurate and unprejudiced attempt to define this novel's different orders of reality. Contrasts Alexander Wedderburn's writing with that of Henry Severell (*The Shadow of the Sun*), of whose art we know little and are permitted to doubt less. In *The Virgin in the Garden* 'the real exists through the mediation of the unreal verbal form', something 'its naturalistic characters are forced to deny' (p. 61).

Fountain, J. Stephen, 'Ashes to Ashes: Kristeva's Jouissance, Alitzer's Apocalypse, Byatt's *Possession* and "The Dream of the Rood" ', *Literature and Theology*, 8/2 (June 1994), 193–208. A difficult but rewarding essay that views our hunger for endings in *Possession* in the context of a post-deconstructionist 'kenotic reading and writing which accepts the end of endings and takes apocalypse seriously, as genesis'.

Franken, Christien, 'Multiple Mythologies: A. S. Byatt and the British Artist-Novel', Ph.D. diss., University of Utrecht, forthcoming. Discusses the relation between art, aesthetics, creativity and gender in *SOS*, *G.* and *P.*, and in her criticism. Contains an extensive primary and secondary bibliography.

Gerrard, Nicci, *Into the Mainstream: How Feminism has Changed Women's Writing* (London: Pandora, 1989). Includes brief passages on Byatt's intellectual and emotional honesty, her compulsion to write unflinchingly on matters of sex and death, and her apprehension of the difficulty of making sense of an entire spectrum of human experience.

Hotho-Jackson, Sabine, 'Literary History in Literature: An Aspect of the Contemporary Novel', *Moderna Sprak*, 86/2 (1992), 113–9. Discussion of *Possession*'s place in a literary tradition that includes John Fowles's *The French Lieutenant's Woman* and Peter Ackroyd's *Hawksmoor*.

Hope, Christopher, and A. S. Byatt, *Contemporary Writers: A. S. Byatt*, pamphlet co-published by Book Trust and the British Council (London, 1990). Includes a tautly sympathetic essay by the novelist Christopher Hope on Byatt's novels up to and including *Possession*.

Hulbert, Ann, 'The Great Ventriloquist: A. S. Byatt's *Possession: A Romance*', in Robert E. Hosmer, Jr (ed.), *Contemporary British Women Writers: Narrative Strategies* (New York: St Martin's Press, 1993), 55–65. Examines the paradoxical coexistence in *Possession* of postmodern ventriloquial knowingness and 'the doubting, inhibited Victorian spirit' (p. 56), arguing that 'lives in the age of sexual ultrasophistication turn out to be frigid, and passion thrives in the age of repression'. Useful bibliography compiled by the editor.

Kenyon, Olga, *Women Novelists Today* (Brighton: Harvester, 1988), 51–84. A theoretically alert chapter that positions Byatt sensitively in terms of her thoughtfulness in the face of the rise of feminism in the 1960s and 1970s, acceding to Byatt's own fear that '[w]hat frightens me is that I'm going to have my interest taken away by women who see literature as a source of interest in women' (pp. 51–84).

Levenson, Michael, 'Essay: The Religion of Fiction'. This review of *Angels and Insects*, which first appeared in the *New Republic*, 2 August 1993, is reprinted as a coda to the reissued edition of A. S. Byatt *Degrees of Freedom* (London: Vintage, 1994), 335–44.

Taylor, D. J., *After the War: The Novel and England since 1945* (London: Chatto & Windus, 1993). Discusses *The Game* and devotes a chapter ('Reading the 1950s', pp. 90–102) to *The Virgin in the Garden* and *Still Life*, arguing their place in Taylor's provocative socio-historical analysis of post-war British fiction.

Todd, Richard, 'The Retrieval of Unheard Voices in British Postmodernist Fiction: A. S. Byatt and Marina Warner', in Theo D'haen and Hans

Bertens (eds.), *Liminal Postmodernisms* (Amsterdam and Atlanta, Ga., 1994), 99–114. Discusses *Possession* and Warner's *Indigo* as sophisticated examples of the literary 'rewriting' of patriarchal tradition.
—— *Consuming Fictions: The Booker Prize and Fiction in Britain Today* (London: Bloomsbury, 1996). Devotes a chapter to an account of the international success of *Possession* in the UK's major export markets and the USA.

TRANSLATIONS

Some readers may be interested in pursuing and consulting translations of Byatt's work. It will be seen that not all the publishers listed below have exclusive rights in a given language. The languages into which more of the work has been translated than any others are Danish and French:

Uitgeverij Altamira (Dutch)
Editorial Anagrama SA (Spanish)
Arcadia (Czech)
Enciclopedia Catalana (Catalan)
Éditions des Cendres (French)
Dong-A Publishing Co (Korean)
Einaudi Editore (Italian)
Flammarion et Cie (French)
Gyldendalske Boghandel (Danish)
Hakusuisha Publishing Co (Japanese)
Hemus (Bulgarian)
Insel Verlag (German)
Companhia das Letras ([Brazilian] Portuguese)
Livanis Publishing (Greek)
Am Oved (Hebrew)
Editions Nephele (Greek)
Pax Publisher (Norwegian)
Rainbow Pocketboeken (Dutch)
Shinchosa Publishers (Japanese)
Shueisha Publishing Inc (Japanese)
SMART Publishing Co (Russian)
Varrak Publishers (Russian)
Wahlstrom & Widstrand (Swedish)
Yapi Kredi Yayinlari (Turkish)

For this information, which is correct at 1 December 1995, I am indebted to the Intercontinental Literary Agency, The Chambers, Chelsea Harbour, Lots Road, London SW10 0XF.

Index

*Recent and
Forthcoming Titles
in the
New Series of*

WRITERS AND
THEIR WORK

WRITERS AND THEIR WORK

RECENT & FORTHCOMING TITLES

TITLES IN PREPARATION

RECENT & FORTHCOMING TITLES

DORIS LESSING
Elizabeth Maslen

Covering a wide range of Doris Lessing's works up to 1992, including all her novels and a selection of her short stories and non-fictional writing, this study demonstrates how Lessing's commitment to political and cultural issues and her explorations of inner space have remained unchanged throughout her career. Maslen also examines Lessing's writings in the context of the work of Bakhtin and Foucault, and of feminist theories.

Elizabeth Maslen is Senior Lecturer in English at Queen Mary and Westfield College, University of London.

0 7463 0705 5 paperback 80pp

JOSEPH CONRAD
Cedric Watts

This authoritative introduction to the range of Conrad's work draws out the distinctive thematic preoccupations and technical devices running through the main phases of the novelist's literary career. Watts explores Conrad's importance and influence as a moral, social and political commentator on his times and addresses recent controversial developments in the evaluation of this magisterial, vivid, complex and problematic author.

"...balanced insights into the controversies surrounding Conrad".
Times Educational Supplement.

Cedric Watts, Professor of English at the University of Sussex, is recognized internationally as a leading authority on the life and works of Joseph Conrad.

0 7463 0737 3 paperback 80pp

JOHN DONNE
Stevie Davies

Raising a feminist challenge to the body of male criticism which congratulates Donne on the 'virility' of his writing, Dr Davies' stimulating and accessible introduction to the full range of the poet's work sets it in the wider cultural, religious and political context conditioning the mind of this turbulent and brilliant poet. Davies also explores the profound emotionalism of Donne's verse and offers close, sensitive readings of individual poems.

Stevie Davies is a literary critic and novelist who has written on a wide range of literature.

0 7463 0738 1 paperback 96pp

THE SENSATION NOVEL
Lyn Pykett

A 'great fact' in the literature of its day, a 'disagreeable' sign of the times, or an ephemeral minor sub-genre? What was the sensation novel, and why did it briefly dominate the literary scene in the 1860s? This wide-ranging study analyses the broader significance of the sensation novel as well as looking at it in its specific cultural context.

Lyn Pykett is Senior Lecturer in English at the University of Wales in Aberystwyth.

0 7463 0725 X paperback 96pp

CHRISTOPHER MARLOWE
Thomas Healy

The first study for many years to explore the whole range of Marlowe's writing, this book uses recent ideas about the relation between literature and history, popular and élite culture, and the nature of Elizabethan theatre to reassess his significance. An ideal introduction to one of the most exciting and innovative of English writers, Thomas Healy's book provides fresh insights into all of Marlowe's important works.

Thomas Healy is Senior Lecturer in English at Birkbeck College, University of London.

0 7463 0707 1 paperback 96pp

ANDREW MARVELL
Annabel Patterson

This state-of-the art guide to one of the seventeenth century's most intriguing poets examines Marvell's complex personality and beliefs and provides a compelling new perspective on his work. Annabel Patterson – one of the leading Marvell scholars – provides comprehensive introductions to Marvell's different self-representations and places his most famous poems in their original context.

Annabel Patterson is Professor of English at Yale University and author of *Marvell and the Civic Crown* (1978).

0 7463 0715 2 paperback 96pp

JOHN CLARE
John Lucas

Setting out to recover Clare – whose work was demeaned and damaged by the forces of the literary establishment – as a great poet, John Lucas offers the reader the chance to see the life and work of John Clare, the 'peasant poet' from a new angle. His unique and detailed study portrays a knowing, articulate and radical poet and thinker writing as much out of a tradition of song as of poetry. This is a comprehensive and detailed account of the man and the artist which conveys a strong sense of the writer's social and historical context.

"Clare's unique greatness is asserted and proved in John Lucas's brilliant, sometimes moving, discourse." **Times Educational Supplement.**

John Lucas has written many books on nineteenth- and twentieth-century literature, and is himself a talented poet. He is Professor of English at Loughborough University.

0 7463 0729 2 paperback 96pp

GEORGE HERBERT
T.S. Eliot
With a new introductory essay by **Peter Porter**

Another valuable reissue from the original series, this important study – one of T. S. Eliot's last critical works – examines the writings of George Herbert, considered by Eliot to be one of the loveliest and most profound of English poets. The new essay by well-known poet and critic Peter Porter reassesses Eliot's study, as well as providing a new perspective on Herbert's work. Together, these critical analyses make an invaluable contribution to the available literature on this major English poet.

0 7463 0746 2 paperback 80pp £5.99

CHILDREN'S LITERATURE
Kimberley Reynolds

Children's literature has changed dramatically in the last hundred years and this book identifies and analyses the dominant genres which have evolved during this period. Drawing on a wide range of critical and cultural theories, Kimberley Reynolds looks at children's private reading, examines the relationship between the child reader and the adult writer, and draws some interesting conclusions about children's literature as a forum for shaping the next generation and as a safe place for developing writers' private fantasies.

"The book manages to cover a surprising amount of ground . . . without ever seeming perfunctory. It is a very useful book in an area where a short pithy introduction like this is badly needed." **Times Educational Supplement**

Kimberley Reynolds lectures in English and Women's Studies at Roehampton Institute, where she also runs the Children's Literature Research Unit.

0 7463 0728 4 paperback 112pp

WILLIAM GOLDING
Kevin McCarron

This comprehensive study takes an interdisciplinary approach to the work of William Golding, placing particular emphasis on the anthropological perspective missing from most other texts on his writings. The book covers all his novels, questioning the status of *Lord of the Flies* as his most important work, and giving particular prominence to *The Inheritors, Pincher Martin, The Spire* and The Sea Trilogy. This in-depth evaluation provides many new insights into the works of one of the twentieth century's greatest writers.

Kevin McCarron is Lecturer in English at Roehampton Institute, where he teaches Modern English and American Literature. He has written widely on the work of William Golding.

0 7463 0735 7 paperback 80pp

WALTER PATER
Laurel Brake

This is the only critical study devoted to the works of Pater, an active participant in the nineteenth-century literary marketplace as an academic, journalist, critic, writer of short stories and novelist. Approaching Pater's writings from the perspective of cultural history, this book covers all his key works, both fiction and non-fiction.

"...grounded in an unmatched scholarly command of Pater's life and writing." **English Association Newsletter**

Laurel Brake is Lecturer in Literature at Birkbeck College, University of London, and has written widely on Victorian literature and in particular on Pater.

0 7463 0716 0 paperback 96pp

ANGELA CARTER
Lorna Sage

Angela Carter was probable the most inventive British novelist of her generation. In this fascinating study, Lorna Sage argues that one of the reasons for Carter's enormous success is the extraordinary intelligence with which she read the cultural signs of our times – from structuralism and the study of folk tales in the 1960s – to, more recently, fairy stories and gender politics. The book explores the roots of Carter's originality and covers all her novels, as well as some short stories and non-fiction.

"...this reappraisal of an interesting novelist explores the roots of her originality . . . a useful introduction to the work of Angela Carter.' **Sunday Telegraph**

Lorna Sage teaches at the University of East Anglia, where she is currently Dean of the School of English and American Studies.

0 7463 0727 6 paperback 96pp

IAN McEWAN
Kiernan Ryan

This is the first book-length study of one of the most original and exciting writers to have emerged in Britain in recent years. It provides an introduction to the whole range of McEwan's work, examining his novels, short stories and screenplays in depth and tracing his development from the 'succès de scandale' of *First Love, Last Rites* to the haunting vision of the acclaimed *Black Dogs*.

"(Written with)...conviction and elegance." **The Irish Times**

Kiernan Ryan is Fellow and Director of Studies in English at New Hall, University of Cambridge.

0 7463 0742 X paperback 80pp

ELIZABETH GASKELL
Kate Flint

Recent critical appraisal has focused on Gaskell both as a novelist of industrial England and on her awareness of the position of women and the problems of the woman writer. Kate Flint reveals how for Gaskell the condition of women was inseparable from broader issues of social change. She shows how recent modes of feminist criticism and theories of narrative work together to illuminate the radicalism and experimentalism which we find in Gaskell's fiction.

Kate Flint is University Lecturer in Victorian and Modern English Literature, and Fellow of Linacre College, Oxford.

0 7463 0718 7 paperback 96pp

KING LEAR
Terence Hawkes

In his concise but thorough analysis of *King Lear* Terence Hawkes offers a full and clear exposition of its complex narrative and thematic structure. By examining the play's central preoccupations and through close analysis of the texture of its verse he seeks to locate it firmly in its own history and the social context to which, clearly, it aims to speak. The result is a challenging critical work which both deepens understanding of this great play and illuminates recent approaches to it.

Terence Hawkes has written several books on both Shakespeare and modern critical theory. He is Professor of English at the University of Wales, Cardiff.

0 7463 0739 X paperback 96pp

JEAN RHYS
Helen Carr

Drawing on her own experience of alienation and conflict as a white-Creole woman, Rhys's novels are recognised as important explorations of gender and colonial power relations. Using feminist and post-colonial theory, Helen Carr's study places Rhys's work in relation to modernist and postmodernist writing and looks closely at how autobiographical material is used by the writer to construct a devastating critique of the greed and cruelty of patriarchy and the Empire.

Helen Carr is Lecturer in English at Goldsmiths College, University of London.

0 7463 0717 9 paperback 96pp

DOROTHY RICHARDSON
Carol Watts

Dorothy Richardson is a major modern novelist whose work is only now beginning to attract the attention of critics, feminists, and cultural theorists. She was one of the earliest novelists to consider the importance of developing a new aesthetic form to represent women's experience and in doing so, she explored many of the new art forms of the twentieth century. Carol Watt's book is an innovative study of her extraordinary thirteen-volume novel, *Pilgrimage* and offers an exciting challenge to the common readings of literary modernism.

Carol Watts is Lecturer in English Literature at Birkbeck College, University of London.

0 7463 0708 X paperback 112pp

APHRA BEHN
Sue Wiseman

Aphra Behn was prolific in all the most commercial genres of her time and wrote widely on many of the most controversial issues of her day – sexual and cultural difference, slavery, politics, and money. Bringing together an analysis of the full range of her writing in poetry, prose and drama, this is the first book-length critical study of Aphra Behn's work, much of which has been hitherto relatively neglected.

Sue Wiseman is Lecturer in English at the University of Warwick.

0 7463 0709 8 paperback 96pp

LEO TOLSTOY
John Bayley

Leo Tolstoy's writing remains as lively, as fascinating, and as absorbing as ever and continues to have a profound influence on imaginative writing. This original and elegant study serves as an introduction to Tolstoy, concentrating on his two greatest novels – *War and Peace* and *Anna Karenina* – and the ancillary texts and tales that relate to them. By examining how Tolstoy created a uniquely spacious and complex fictional world, John Bayley provides a fascinating analysis of the novels, explaining why they continue to delight and inform readers today.

John Bayley is Warton Professor of English Emeritus at St Catherine's College, University of Oxford.

0 7463 0744 6 paperback 96pp

EDMUND SPENSER
Colin Burrow

Considered by many to be the greatest Elizabethan poet, Edmund Spenser's writing has inspired both admiration and bewilderment. The grace of Spenser's language and his skilful and enchanting evocation of the fairy world have, for many, been offset by the sheer bulk and complexity of his work. Colin Burrow's considered and highly readable account provides a reading of Spenser which clarifies the genres and conventions used by the writer. Burrow explores the poet's taste for archaism and allegory, his dual attraction to images of vital rebirth and mortal frailty, and his often conflictual relationship with his Queen and with the Irish landscape in which he spent his mature years.

Colin Burrow is Fellow, Tutor and College Lecturer in English at Gonville & Caius College, University of Cambridge.

0 7463 0750 0 paperback 128pp

HENRY FIELDING
Jenny Uglow

In this fresh introduction to his work, Uglow looks at Fielding in his own historical context and in the light of recent critical debates. She identifies and clarifies many of Fielding's central ideas, such as those of judgement, benevolence and mercy which became themes in his novels. Looking not only at the novels, but also at Fielding's drama, essays, journalism and political writings, Uglow traces the author's development, clarifies his ideas on his craft, and provides a fascinating insight into eighteenth-century politics and society.

Jenny Uglow is a critic and publisher.

0 7463 0751 9 paperback 96pp

HENRY JAMES
The Later Writing
Barbara Hardy

Barbara Hardy focuses on Henry James's later works, dating from 1900 to 1916. Offering new readings of the major novels and a re-evaluation of the criticism to date, she considers language and theme in a number of Jamesian works, including *The Ambassadors, The Wings of the Dove* and *The Golden Bowl*, and engages with his autobiographical and travel writing and literary criticism. Hardy's analysis traces two dominant themes – the social construction of character and the nature of creative imagination – and reveals James to be a disturbing analyst of inner life.

Barbara Hardy is Professor Emeritus at Birkbeck College, University of London.

0 7463 0748 9 paperback 96pp

DAVID LODGE
Bernard Bergonzi

Internationally celebrated as both a novelist and a literary critic, David Lodge is one of Britain's most successful and influential living writers. He has been instrumental in introducing and explaining modern literary theory to British readers while maintaining, in regard to his own work, "faith in the future of realistic fiction". Bergonzi's up-to-date and comprehensive study covers both Lodge's critical writing as well as his novels of the past 35 years (from *The Picturegoers* to *Therapy*) and explores how he expresses and convincingly combines metafiction, realism, theology and dazzling comedy.

Bernard Bergonzi is Emeritus Professor of English at the University of Warwick.

0 7463 0755 1 paperback 80pp

DAVID HARE
Jeremy Ridgman

David Hare is one of the most prolific, challenging, and culturally acclaimed playwrights in Britain today. Jeremy Ridgman's study focuses on the dramatic method that drives the complex moral and political narratives of Hare's work. He considers its relationship to its staging and performance, looking in particular at the dramatist's collaborations with director, designer, and performer. Hare's writing for the theatre since 1970 is set alongside his work for television and film and his achievements as director and translator, to provide a detailed insight into key areas of his dramatic technique particularly dialogue, narrative, and epic form.

Jeremy Ridgman is Senior Lecturer in the Department of Drama and Theatre Studies at Roehampton Institute, London

0 7463 0774 8 paperback 96pp

TONY HARRISON
Joe Kelleher

Tony Harrison has been acclaimed worldwide, not only for his slim volumes of poetry but also for his lyric sequences and long poems, for his adaptations and original plays for the theatre, his opera libretti, and his verse films for television. Kelleher argues that Harrison's unique achievement is to ransack a whole range of traditions in order to carve out in verse, a very innovative and contemporary mode of public utterance.

Joe Kelleher is a playwright and Lecturer in Drama at Roehampton Institute.

0 7463 0789 6 paperback 96pp

CHARLOTTE YONGE
Alethea Hayter

Charlotte Yonge was a best-selling Victorian author and widely admired by her greatest literary contemporaries in the mid-ninteenth century but for the next hundred years, ignored or vilified by critics. Her work has only recently begun to receive the attention it deserves from biographers, historians and feminists. Alethea Hayter's appraisal of Yonge as a writer surveys the full range of her work – her non-fictional studies in history and wild-life, as well as her family chronicles, historical novels and children's books. Yonge emerges as a perceptive writer who well deserves the renewed interest in her and her work.

Alethea Hayter is a literary critic and historian, who has pubished a number of books on nineteenth-century literature.

0 7463 0781 0 paperback 96pp